THE NOVICHOK CHRONICLES

The Skripal and Navalny Hoaxes Compared

THE NOVICHOK CHRONICLES

By Nick Kollerstrom PhD

ISBN 978-1-7399994-1-4

2nd Edition 2022

Other books by the author:

Terror on the Tube, Behind the Veil of 7/7 – an Investigation 2012
How Britain Initiated both World Wars 2017
False flags over Europe – A Modern history of State-Fabricated Terror 2018
Who did 9/11? A view from across the Pond 2019
The Great British Coronavirus Hoax 2020

Acknowledgements: thanks to Stephen Windsor-Clive for insightful editing work and Simon Day for cover design.

Contents

A Prelude To WW3

In 2014 The distinguished German journalist Udo Ofkotte was an editor for *Frankfurter Algemeine Zeitung* one of Europe's largest newspapers, when he published his bestselling book *Presstitutes* (English translation). A couple of years later he explained to RT that he had been driven to speak out, because of the way in which anti-Russian propaganda had become compulsory:

> I've been a journalist for about 25 years, and I was educated to lie, to betray, and not to tell the truth to the public.... But seeing right now within the last months how the German and American media tries to bring war to the people of Europe, to bring war to Russia – this is a point of no return and I'm going to stand up and say it is not right what my colleagues do and have done in the past because they are bribed to betray the people, not only in Germany, all over Europe. The reason for writing this book is that I am very fearful of a new war in Europe...I have just written in the book how we have betrayed our readers in the past just to push for war... If you see the German media, especially my colleagues who day by day write against the Russians...

Shortly after that interview he died of a 'heart attack,' aged 56. Thus he paid the ultimate price for giving to the world this message. Let us take good notice of it, as we are now verily drifting towards this 'new war in Europe.' Can we appreciate his wise words? This book examines one thread of the fictional propaganda that is now leading us to this end, this terrible end.

Julian Assange has also paid a high price for his message, for his attempt to improve journalism by an open information policy. He said in an interview,

> most wars are a result of media lies. One of the hopeful things that I've discovered is that nearly every war that has started in the last fifty years has been a result of media lies. The media could have stopped it if they'd searched deep enough. If they hadn't reprinted

government propaganda they could have stopped it. What does that mean? That means, basically populations don't like wars and populations have to be fooled into wars..

How true! In the year 2017, Theresa May officially declared that Britain had got an enemy. Who might that be? She, as Britain's Prime Minister, advised a major Euro-forum who it had to hate – why Russia, once again![1] To a European Union summit meeting she averred, "We must be open-eyed to the actions of hostile states like Russia which … attempt to tear our collective strength apart"[2] and assigned *a hundred million pound* funding to promote negative coverage of the Russian state, both in Russia and neighboring countries – to be spent over the next five years.

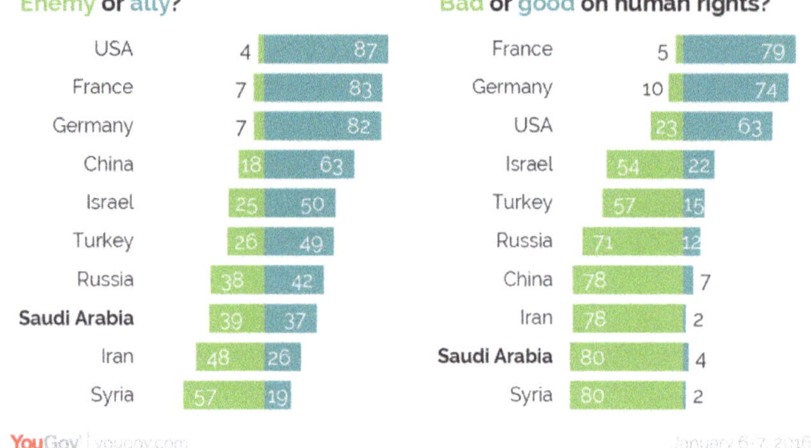

Figure: A 2020 survey, showing Russia not generally seen as a threat

We the British people never asked for that, with polls showing that Russia was mostly not viewed as a threat. But the warmongers needed some new challenge, as if merely bombing Islamic nations which could

[1] Euobserver.com 'UK to call out 'hostile' Russia at EU summit'.24.11.17

[2] 24.11.17, May at Eastern Partnership Summit in Brussels, averring Russia aimed to 'sow discord' and of course promote 'fake news.'

not defend themselves was not enough. Her statement came four months *before* the Skripal event, at which time the British people were far from acknowledging that Russia had again become 'the Enemy.'[3] That hundred million pounds was spent in a secret, covert manner to teach people how to hate Russia.[4]

This secret, multi-million-pound initiative was to extend over several years with no public oversight. But disclosures leaked out as regards how the funding had been used and they revealed, as a shocked RT journalist commented:

> … the extraordinary lengths London is determined to go to in service of demonizing, destabilizing and isolating Russia nationally and internationally… For all the mainstream media's alarmist chatter of the threat of Kremlin *"disinformation"*, not a single example of anything even remotely comparable to the full-spectrum, multi-channel, on - and offline, global assault on perceptions outlined in this article has ever been attributed to Moscow, or any other *"hostile"* state.[5]

Britain's military expenditure soared in late 2020 by an extra £16 billion yearly, putting it temporarily above that of Russia.[6] Why would a small country protected by seas with no enemy need so vast a military expenditure, equal to that for the whole of Russia? In March 2021 a massive increase in the number of UK nuclear warheads was announced, from its former goal-number of 180 right up to 260 by the middle of the decade, with no explanation of the overriding of previous pledges given to reduce that number and work towards a nuclear-free world. The UK already had more than enough nuclear warheads to destroy all of the capital cities of Earth, so what was the point? Whatever you think the answer may be, such huge expenditure and increase of nuclear warheads clearly necessitates some intense demonizing of whoever the enemy is

---

[3] rt.com 'Leaked papers allege massive UK govt effort to co-opt Russian-language anti-Kremlin media & influencers to 'weaken Russian state.' 18.2.21

[4] For the mass of documents now leaked see 'HMG Trojan Horse. Part 4: Undermining Russia II' 4.2.21

[5] Kit Clarenberg on rt.com, 'Leaked papers allege massive UK govt effort to co-opt Russian-language anti-Kremlin media & influencers to 'weaken Russian state' 18.2.2021 (See also his articles in thegrayzone.com)

[6] UK military expenditure 2021 $55bn, Russia 3.11 tr Rubles = $40bn, source worldpopulationreview.com, 'Military Spending by Country.' 2021,

perceived to be.

For plutonium to be brewed up, purified and put into the Trident nuclear sub warheads, a strong and resilient enemy-image has to exist. Who thinks we need more nuclear warheads? *Homo Exterminans* – to coin a phrase - will explain this to you in a clear and logical way. I may be echoing E.P.Thompson's 1980 *Exterminism and Cold War,* which envisaged 'exterminism' as a condition whereby the military-industrial complex has grown so powerful that it was able to condition what politicians were able to say and do. Theresa May's announcement of the new enemy came within a year or so of Udo Ofkotte's revelation of how a new enemy-image had to be brewed up - evidence of the Deep State working.

Alas, the words written by Machiavelli five centuries ago remain all too relevant:

> I say ... that governments should fear those persons who make war their only business...No-one can be called a good man who in order to support himself, takes up a profession that obliges him to be at all times rapacious, fraudulent and cruel...' (*The Art of War*)

We need to appreciate that military intelligence is a contradiction in terms: the military *don't have intelligence,* they're killers, trained to obey and kill.

In September 2020, as small businesses were closing down at an unprecedented rate in the midst of the coronavirus lockdown, did *anyone* approve of that huge hike in military expenditure? Were there not better ways to spend it? That was a theft of billions from hardworking taxpayers struggling to make a living, to pay for more Trident nuclear warheads.

Who Needs an Enemy?

The Greek myth of *Europa and the Bull* depicts the soul of Europe, *Europa* being carried off and raped by a raging bull - which today has to represent the military - industrial complex. Let us never forget Eisenhower's most prophetic of closing speeches when he gave the stark, clear warning of what lay ahead for future generations in the West if we allowed this very menace unchained to dominate our existence – in all it's psychopathic, vaulting ambition. Arise, citizens of England, and say No to the warmongers!

Thus far, in the 21st century 'Islamic terror' had been hyped as the new enemy: after all, had not Muslims done 9/11? Was that not enough, and did we also need to have Russia as an enemy? It had never desired to attack the UK in its entire history. Who had decided all of this?

The 'Axis of Evil' was properly defined in the year 2011, by me, as follows: 'The Axis of Evil US-UK is white, from Whitehall to the White House, and its holy-communion taking leaders go about their normal business of stealing the resources, demonizing and bombing nations of darker skin color.'[7] That Axis is, in this 21st century, fully dedicated to Eternal War.

The 'Enemy' was at that time Islamic. Complicated state-fabricated terror events or more usually mock-terror events (actors and dummies etc.) have been in this century designed and enacted, to project huge waves of fear and despair into the people and destroy their faith in human nature, in order to ratify the bombing of Islamic nations and especially their capital cities: Baghdad, Tripoli, Damascus. I've done several books on this subject.[8]

Here are the primary false-flag terror events of Europe in this 21st century - with apologies to the reader for so brusque an outline - those staged in England being highlighted in red. All but one (the MH17 shootdown) were blamed upon Muslims:

> Madrid train bombings, 2004 * **London 7/7 bombings, 2005** * **Heathrow liquid bomb hoax 2006** * Crotch bomber at Amsterdam airport, 2009 * Norway Utoya Island massacre, 2011 * **the Woolwich Terror hoax 2013** * Ukraine MH17 shootdown, 2013 * Paris, Charlie Hebdo 2015 * Bataclan, Paris hit by fictional terror, 2016 * Mock Terror in Brussels airport, 2016 * Nice, Munich & Mossad 2016 * **Phantom terror over Westminster Bridge, 2017 * Fake terror at Manchester arena concert, 2017**.

The earlier events featured real deaths while later ones were done with crisis actors and dummies. For full details see my *False Flags over Europe A Modern History of State-fabricated Terror* (2020), wherein each of the above highly deceptive events is assigned a chapter. *Five* of them were staged in England, revealing how Britain has become an epicentre of this horrific new art-form.

---

[7] NK, *Terror on the Tube, Behind the Veil of 7/7 an Investigation*,2009, p.262.

[8] Ibid, also NK, *False Flags over Europe A Modern History of State-Fabricated Terror*, 2018 and *Who did 9/11, A View from Across the Pond*, 2021.

The British people are not interested in this fact and my opus has received no media coverage.

Comment upon this list of thirteen state-fabricated terror events would be an undue digression. But the list serves to indicate the dreadful skill which British Intelligence has acquired in the Black Arts of deception, and also to show how the sequence terminated in the year 2017. They weren't required any more, once Theresa May had that year announced the new Enemy.

State-fabricated terror *cannot be discussed* by any politician simply because the state risks everything by doing such a thing, it would itself collapse – or morph into something quite dire – if its own role in the events became evident: for example the British army's role in the Skripal event. The present work concerns certain truths which no politician is allowed to mention. Now that is quite an interesting situation. It would help their grasp of what is happening in the world if they did comprehend these issues but one appreciates that they cannot be spoken.

In George Orwell's *1984* there is a scene where the people are collectively expressing their daily hate towards one country (Oceana) and it is then shifted over to another power-bloc (Eurasia) and nobody seems to mind. The important thing is that there is an Enemy. That is *precisely* what happened in the middle of the second decade of this 21st century. One had assumed that the post-9/11 list of seven to-be-bombed Islamic nations[9] was enough to satisfy the Military-Industrial Complex at least for a while, but no. Abruptly and seemingly out of the blue, Russia re-emerged as the new enemy *du jour*. The big state-fabricated terror events climaxed abruptly in the year 2017 (the Westminster Bridge story, then the Manchester Arena fabricated mock-terror events – I devote lengthy chapters to each of them – both blamed upon a lone-nut Muslim), then for the last five years we haven't had any.

State-fabricated, false-flag terror means that such events are 'false-flag' in that the blame is intended to fall upon an innocent third party, which has now become Russia, and 'state- fabricated' means that the police cannot and will not ever solve them - because the government is complicit. It is a post-9/11 form of political theatre, a straight-from-Hell art-form that has developed in this 21st century, even though it did to

---

[9] The seven (Muslim) nations to be 'taken out' post-9/11 by America were Iraq, Syria, Lebanon, Libya, Somalia, Sudan and Iran. See NK *Who did 9/11?*, 2021, p.238.

some degree exist in earlier times.

So we can all forget about Islamic terror. Hooray we've got a new enemy, and yes its big, bad old Russia. I once asked a historian if there was a time when Britain had managed to get by without having an external, foreign enemy with whom were at war or at least had to hate and fear. His eyes glazed over for a while then he said, yes maybe there had been a brief period sometime before the Napoleonic wars…

The 'Axis of Evil' is properly threefold – US, Israel and the UK– and it works synergistically such that the different elements can hardly be separated out. For example the assassination of Lady Di, Our Princess, on 30th of August 1997, was by that trio each having their own motive and no-one (I believe) can disentangle their relative contributions to what took place, under the Pons d'Alma bridge as she hit the 13th column.[10] She was too independent, too beautiful and was about to marry a Muslim. Mull over this next time you watch a James Bond film.

A country has wisdom if it is capable of living without war. That, gentle reader, does not apply to the nation which we presently inhabit. On the contrary we are on a kind of road to Hell, in which Untruth normally hits the headlines.

The Need for Nightmares

This work is a study of British intelligence and the skill it has acquired over the last century in constructing *war-ratifying illusions*. The big question one wants to ask is, 'Why would it want to do that?' *Cui bono* and to whose advantage is it to live in a culture of lies and intrigue fostered by such 'Dark Arts'? That *the people have to live in fear* turns out to be a very fundamental axiom of politics in this century. For the RAF to bomb the cities of other nations, it is required that the British people must approve or at any rate not dissent and so the fear-porn images are rolled out to that end. That is the purpose of state fabricated terror.[11]

Ultimate evil in this 21st century has some straightforward

---

[10] *Princess Diana the Hidden Evidence* by Jon King and John Beveridge 2002 is not a bad place to start.

[11] In *False Flags over Europe, A Modern history of state-Fabricated Terror* (2018) I alluded to '…state-fabricated terror events, now appearing as *the primary art-form* of the 21st century,' p.237.

characteristics: it works through deception and untruth, it promotes militarism and war and it works to extinguish whatever hopes the human race might have had for a better tomorrow. It always works through the emotions of hate and fear.

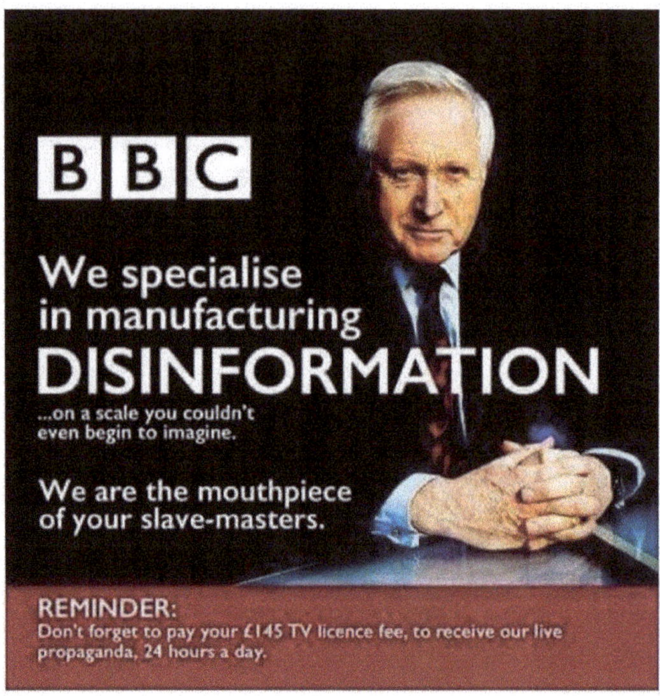

Those who Create Delusion ensure that human beings spend much of their life fearing that which has no reality but only a mere semblance of being. *Homo exterminans* are those who promote this enterprise. They are indeed the Enemies of Mankind. They work through the *logic of mirror-delusion,* projecting upon the Other what they are themselves doing. Are we here talking about the well – meaning, well -educated chaps at the F.O.? Yes, indeed. The webs of deception are not really woven by outright liars: those involved do in some degree believe in what they are promoting although at the back of their mind will be Churchillian warmonger dictum 'Truth is so precious that it has to be protected by a bodyguard of lies.'

NATO Yearning for WW3

Peace in Europe *can only exist* if citizens trouble to seek out truthful narratives which can expose the war-ratifying work of those who create the great deceptions. That is our 21st-century reality. This may sound conspiratorial and indeed it is. When such huge military budgets are involved and large standing armies mill about, a theatre of untruth to create fear and hate does inevitably develop, under the guise of a false patriotism. Do we get to listen to the Other's point of view when the BBC demonizes any group of people?

We will see how the outrageous untruths and half-truths emerging from NATO's 'heart of darkness' may remind us that *Operation Gladio* has not altogether died. Readers may wish to peruse Richard Cottrell's excellent *Gladio: NATO's Dagger at the Heart of Europe* (2015).[12] Gladio was a last-century operation, based on the notion that citizens did not sufficiently fear the enemy from which NATO was supposedly protecting them and so mockup events had to be created to instil such fear. The Skripal and Navalny events have a distinct *Gladio* flavour to them.

In futurity, experts combing the radioactive ruins of Europe may wonder why NATO wished to abandon its defensive function as enshrined in the 1949 North Atlantic Treaty, whereby it existed to prevent another war in Europe: instead it spent decades pushing more and more high-powered military hardware ever closer to the borders of Russia. Was not anyone bothered by the way America had a vastly different perspective on war in Europe, to the Europeans? It had after all benefitted greatly from the previous two world wars.

The definitive transform came in 1999 with the breakup of Yugoslavia, when without a UN Security Council resolution and in direct violation of the Helsinki Accords NATO bombed a sovereign state for three months, killing 1,700 civilians. The founding principle of a defensive alliance had thus been trashed, i.e. it was no longer governed by the North Atlantic Treaty. Are not Europeans frightened by this vast alliance with its 'open-door' policy of admitting new members, no coherent governing principles and its fixed enemy-image of Russia as the bad guy? Where do they imagine it will end?

It would be true to say that the Warsaw Pact (1955-1991) kept the peace in Europe as long as it lived.

---

[12] The other essential work here is Daniel Ganser, *NATO's Secret Armies*, 2007.

For the last thirty years Europe has been free from the terror of nuclear war. Whereas earlier, in the 1980s, polls had shown how a *majority* of the populations of European nations had been expecting nuclear war. That fear faded away because real diplomats had worked hard and established the INF treaty – banning all 'Intermediate-Range' nuclear weapons from Europe. All those awful cruise missiles etc were removed. But, that treaty was allowed to expire in 2019 and such intermediate-range nuclear weapons are now being re-installed in Germany, Poland and Rumania. Russia will then reluctantly have to set up corresponding nuke missiles pointing at Germany. Are Europeans bothered by this? Have you heard any European politicians express concern about this? Not at all. Never.

Only the Russians, Putin and Lavrov, have expressed their grave concern. In the year 2001 Putin said at a German conference (speaking in German) *"I cannot imagine my own country in isolation from Europe and the so-called civilized world, so it's hard for me to view NATO as an enemy."* He became the founder of a new 'Common European Home' ideology -which has failed of course. It was *made to fail.*

There remained a slender ray of hope that friendship rather than war might prevail in Europe and that came from the Nordstream-II pipeline. For that reason both the UK and US were instructing Germany to scrap it as the hour of its completion drew near. Never mind that Germany had asked for it in the first place, never mind the twenty billion Euros spent in its construction, never mind how greatly it is needed after Germany decommissioned its nuclear power plants and closing its coal mines. Germany is still an occupied country with no peace treaty having been signed at the end of WW2 and with plenty of US-UK troops and military bases present, to remind them that it does not have its own sovereignty. One thing which the Axis of Evil US-UK simply cannot allow is, friendship developing between Germany and Russia. NATO exists in order to prevent this:

> American colleagues at the Pentagon told me, unequivocally, that the US and UK never would allow European-Soviet (re: EU-Russia) relations to develop to such a degree that they would challenge the US-UK's political, economic or military primacy and hegemony on the European continent. Such a development will be prevented by all necessary means, if necessary by provoking a war

in central Europe. Christof Lehmann[13]

- Thus, many believe that the threats of war over Ukraine were designed to prevent the tap being turned on: that if only Russia could be provoked into some incident there, then Germany could be persuaded not to use the Pipeline (which has now clearly happened, as of 22.2.22).

By the same token, friendship between these two nations is what the world needs most if we are ever to have a world living in peace - if one can even attempt to imagine such a thing. We'll see how the Novichok Part II story – the Navalny episode – became located in Germany, or endeavoured to locate itself in Germany, for this very reason.

Its not hard to guess why Russia is being hated and demonized so intensely. It is after all a Christian nation, in which thousands of new churches are being built and three-quarters of its population identify themselves as Orthodox Christian. It will be the nation where the white race survives, as Europe and America go brown. Worst of all, it refuses to promote sodomy nor will it even allow schoolteachers to molest children's genitals or give them hormone sex-change therapy. These things do indeed provoke the *rage of the Empire.*

But perhaps worse than any of these things is the way Putin has set up the independent BRICS banking system, signed on 16 July 2014 the very day before the MH-17 shootdown. To quote the geopolitical analyst Webster Tarpley, 'MH-17 is the US-UK answer to launch of BRICS bank at Fortaleze summit – the biggest challenge to IMF and World Bank since 1944.' BRICS is a pacific alliance, concerned to develop mutual trade, prosperity and cultural exchange, enough said.

Russians have been and are quite scrupulous about adherence to treaties and international law agreements, and the West in the last century did once have diplomats who shared that attitude. However such treaties tend to involve long sentences with subordinate clauses, conditional tenses and such like, which today's Euro-politicians may find hard to handle. They prefer short phrases like 'build back better' and will quickly dismiss any discourse outside the approved party line with snappy phrases like 'disinformation,' 'conspiracy theory' or 'Kremlin propaganda.'

---

[13] Quoted by Mike Whitney in unz.com, 'will Washington launch a Mass-Casualty 'false-flag' to sabotage Nord Stream? 17.2.22.

For example NATO is supposedly held together by its article 5, 'An attack on one is an attack on all.' That is a short enough sentence to remain current, and does it mean that America would go to war for the sake of Montenegro? Would Americans agree to war for a country they cannot find on the map? That's what it means and if it doesn't mean that then it doesn't mean anything. Its thirty nations now are being held together primarily by its defined enemy image, which initially it wasn't supposed to have.

An Art of Deception

The Western society may have accustomed itself to this kind of media shenanigans. They probably realize what's happening and think nothing can be done about this global-scale deceit, but we disagree. We don't want to live in a kingdom of crooked mirrors. We won't put up with these endless lies. Maria Zakharova , spokesperson for Russia's Foreign Ministry, *20.2.22*

As the world recovered from lockdown and we were trying to remember what normal life was like, one sensed a distinct 'chill in the air' of European politics. People were suddenly expecting a war to come in Europe and it seems to be accepted that our enemy is Russia, when one had supposed the cold war to be a thing of the past... gone like the Berlin wall. What in recent years has happened we ask, to bring this about? We return to the question, why now is this great nation in the cross-hairs once again after we all thought we'd arrived at a precious and lasting détente?

We will be examining three *venomous* (in every sense of the word) stories which share allegations of Russian guilt. They concern an unimaginable horror and that is the use of unseen and invisible chemical weapons. The stories are *sequential* in that each builds upon the previous one. None have been proven or established, as a court of law would demand, and each is constructed to designate guilt upon a chosen enemy.

As a science historian I have focused upon the factual details of the narratives, but the bigger picture of why it is all happening may be more important and that is much harder to evaluate. One startling feature of the present threefold tale is the expulsion of diplomats. That was a consequence, once NATO and the European Parliament came to accept – without any coherent debate - the constructed Russia-did-it poison narratives formulated by the US/UK military intelligence. Thereby we have arrived at Cold War 2.0, however let's recall that the cold war of thirty years ago had diplomats who were able to manage it and ensure that it did not warm unduly. That, today, is very much lacking.

In order for diplomats to have any control over how events unfold, some attempt at a truthful narrative is required, so that negotiations can maintain peace which is and always has been the remit of diplomacy. In the context of the three staged events here evaluated, there is a need for discussion forums to be set up to try and ascertain 'What Really Happened,' or to get as near to it as possible. We need to establish, as our right in a democracy and with the help of a decent media who actually understand their job, these things.

'Did they mislead us, the quiet - voiced elders?' asked the poet, T.S. Eliot. Well, yes, I'm afraid they did. Whether it's the shootdown of MH-17 over Ukraine or the Alexei Navalny story, it is only the power and authority of truthful narratives that can rescue us now. With sorrow we witness how the intelligent and tactful business of diplomacy is being all too easily replaced by name-calling and insult. Diplomacy involves seeing the point of view of the Other and that is the last thing desired by the US/UK military intelligences, whose main aim is always to promote the Threat, the Enemy over there, and thereby obtain their shiny new hardware.

A Sequential trio of Illusions

It was evidently not enough for half a dozen Islamic nations to have been bombed back into the stone age. After all, they have the oil, opium, lithium etc... We look at the demonising of Russia that has taken place through three *fictionally constructed events*: Litvinenko (2006), Skripal (2018), Navalny (2020), examining how the western media have swallowed these improbable, half - baked narratives without proper question or debate. Great achievements of the 20th century - East-West detente, mutual understanding, dialogue, trade and cultural exchange - have been rendered obsolete by a Churchillian - type logic of imperial hubris: where illusion and lies become essential components in the promotion of conflict.

The sequence of illusions we here examine was brewed up by the US-UK *Axis of Evil* and each successfully *projected blame* onto Russia. Each used an evil-sounding and unheard-of poison, polonium-210 for Litvinenko in 2006 then Novichok for the Skripals on March 4, 2018 and Alexei Navalny in August, 2020. Large European institutions such as the EU and the ECHR (European Council for Human Rights) then endorse these hate-generating, unproven narratives.

As we drift towards World War Three, to be fought once again in Europe, it may be worth deconstructing them. For indeed, only the truth can save us now.

Where it begins: Litvinenko, 2006

Official statements about the Skripal story normally allude to the earlier poisoning story of 2006, as being the warrant for blame to be cast upon Russia. Through studying the similarities between the Skripal and Navalny narratives, we can appreciate the deep significance of that earlier event. It was in truth their progenitor.

That Litvinenko story took years to gestate, with something resembling an inquest only happening in 2012 under ultra-secret conditions. It found Russian guilt to be 'strongly suspected,' being set up to do just that. That theme of Russian guilt began on November 19th of 2006 when the Russian billionaire dissident Boris Berezovsky announced to the newspapers that he believed Vladimir Putin was behind the poisoning of his employee Alexei Litvinenko, as the latter lay dying in a hospital bed.

A few days later experts averred that the death had been caused by the rare and exotic polonium-210. This was pretty well unheard-of as a poison: a mere microgram or so had done it, allegedly costing millions of dollars. Special alpha-radiation detectors had ascertained this, we were told. Who could have wanted to do this or afford to buy the polonium? What had been the point? One thing was for sure, it grabbed the headlines.

Experts from the Atomic Energy Authority were able to use their alpha- and gamma-radiation detecting equipment, and detected it in his hair, blood and urine. Later on the whole story expanded to have polonium detected on passenger planes, hotel rooms etc and again we're left wondering how this was done - if indeed it was.

After accusing Russia, the British authorities *refused* Russian requests for the polonium evidence. We're reminded of the later Novichok accusations where Russian requests for collaboration were likewise refused. Retro-scepticism tends to impinge upon this case: as the Skripal story involved Novichok being detected in all sorts of places – a house, a car, a restaurant, the hotel room of the two suspects, only announced by the police six months later and quite unknown to the hotel owner, which seems doubtful - so likewise this earlier polonium-trail that was found to be all over the place - supposedly marking out the journeys of the two chief suspects - is open to doubt.

A pre-set narrative was rolled out like a James Bond story, as citizens were thrilled to hear about those *evil Russkies* roaming the streets of London with deadly polonium-210. At no point did any police or criminal court ascertain that an act of murder had been committed: it was presupposed and became the official narrative as the media went along with it. The man who found himself accused – now a quite eminent member of the Russian parliament - was puzzled as to what motive he was supposed to have had, to poison his old friend.

'Putin, Putin' screeched the media, and journalist William Dunkerley found it strange that the Russian president failed to defend himself: "The problem is that for far too long Putin has allowed his enemies to define him. They've been in control of his image"[14] There was the` usual deep silence from the Russian side when we most need a reply or explanation: but, perhaps they were just as puzzled as anyone. Again William Dunkerley wondered:

> If the truth has been on Putin's side, how come his enemies have succeeded in destroying his reputation so thoroughly? Putin's political enemies effectively weaponised the media to attack his reputation. That's how. They engaged in highly sophisticated media manipulation. And Putin put up no defence. He let them get away with it.[15]

That is a story we'll see repeatedly.

---

[14] Dunkerley, *Ukraine in the Crosshairs* 2014, p.160

[15] Dunkerley, *Litvineko Murder Case Solved,* 2015 p200.

After years of mysterious and unexplained delay, a non-public Enquiry was opened up, chaired by Lord Owen. His Report explained why the likes of you and I could not be entrusted to hear the evidence:

> Put very shortly, the closed evidence consists of evidence that is relevant to the Inquiry, but which has been assessed as being too sensitive to put into the public domain. The assessment that the material is sufficiently sensitive to warrant being treated as closed evidence in these proceedings has been made not by me, but by the Home Secretary. She has given effect to this decision by issuing a number of Restriction Notices, which is a procedure specified in section 19 of the Inquiries Act 2005. The Restriction Notices themselves, although not, of course, the sensitive documents appended to them, are public documents. They have been published on the Inquiry website and are also to be found at Appendix 7 to this Report.

Concerning this cover-up during the death Enquiry, Dunkerley reached the pessimistic conclusion:

> The record has become confounded by lies and fabricated stories. They've apparently permeated the official case. There is little chance of ever finding the truth. The honest course would be to admit that the truth is unattainable, and just dismiss the case and avoid further embarrassment.[16]

… well that definitely wasn't going to happen. Years later in September of 2021 the European Court of Human Right re-hashed the British story, finding Russia guilty and demanding that it pay compensation to the widow of Litvinenko! In its judgement the Court was, in the words of one lawyer 'reversing the burden of proof' i.e. it cited no evidence.[17] It reiterated the improbable British teapot story: "When putting the poison in the teapot from which Mr Litvinenko poured a drink, they knew that, once ingested, the poison would kill Mr Litvinenko" – words may fail us at this point, but see the next chapter.

---

[16] Dunkerley, *Op. Cit.*, 2015, p.158.

[17] Marco Milanovic, Professor of Public international Law at U. of Nottingham: ejiltalk.org/european-court-finds-russia-assassinated-alexander-litvinenko/

Sergei Skripal and his daughter

In 2018, Two Russians were captured and abducted in the town of Salisbury, from which a vast Euro-narrative was developed. Blame was skillfully projected onto Russians thousands of miles away. Complicated discussions took place in European institutions about 'Novichok' from which Russia was excluded, its blame and guilt being pre-ordained.

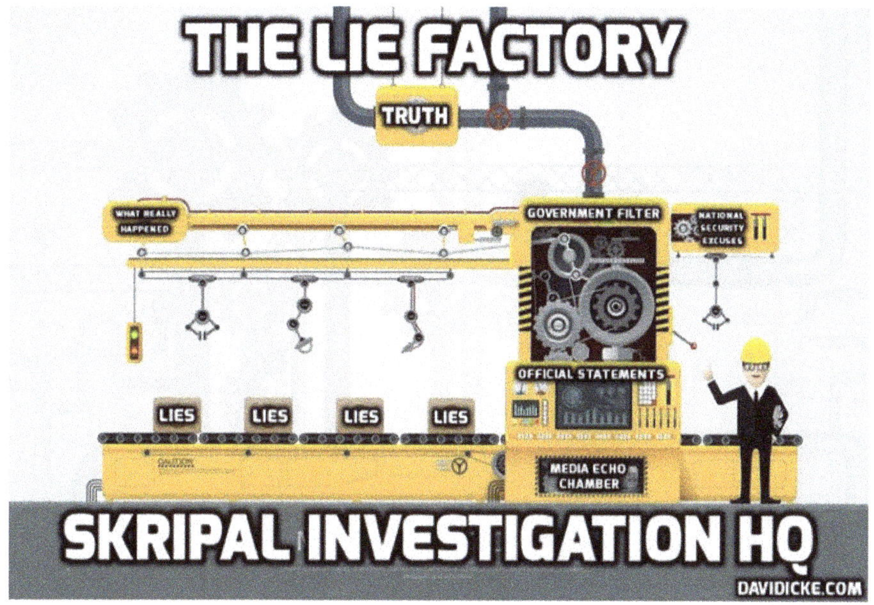

Figure: David Icke's view of the Skripal narrative

The poisoning of the two Skripals became the main news story of 2018, the year Before Covid. A crime had been committed – two Russians were abducted by the British government and effectively *imprisoned,* since when none of their friends or relatives have ever seen them. But in addition the victims were *us, we the public,* as we were traumatized and impacted by the story, of what did *not* happen. We are also taught who to hate – the evil Russkies, of course.

The British Government now uses names like *Institute for Statecraft* and *Integrity Initiative* for blatantly warmongering anti-Russian mendacity. To quote Craig Murray here, "if the *Integrity Initiative* is promoting it, you know it is not true."[18] The US journalist Max

[18] Craig Murray, 'Ten Points I just can't Believe about the Official Skripal Story,' point no. 1, 7.3.19.

Blumenthal alludes to the secretive manner in which UK government has funded deep-state militarism and started a new Cold War (see tweet). Ordinary folk watching the news do not suspect that Government-funded groups like these are involved in constructing and promoting the fake Skripal poisoning narrative.

Max Blumenthal
@MaxBlumenthal

Replying to @MaxBlumenthal

The Integrity Initiative is just a small gear in a semi-covert military-intel & corporate backed op spanning Western govs, NGO's & media. This propaganda machine was built to hype a new Cold War, ramp up military spending & undermine any politician or critic who gets in the way.

433 10:00 PM - Dec 18, 2018

323 people are talking about this

It would be hard imagine a more absurd story than that put out concerning the Skripals in Salisbury: two unseen Russians skulk up to their front door, when both Sergei and Yulia Skripal were at home, and smear 'Novichok' on the front door handle, then three hours after leaving home the two Skripals collapse synchronously onto a park bench - *after* they had fed the ducks, had a meal at Zizzi's restaurant and enjoyed a glass of beer! Really, people said, could not MI5 have dreamed up a better story than that?

The people of Salisbury would surely find that their morale and social cohesiveness much improved were they to express their indignation and insist on a public enquiry into What Really Happened. They have been stressed and traumatized as their town was impacted by *fictional horror* - courtesy of their own Government. It would help if they could to start a campaign themed around e.g. 'Where is Yulia?' - 'Release Yulia' - 'We demand to see Yulia!' in case she is still alive. May 11th as the date of Yulia's last 'appearance' could be an anniversary date, or perhaps the 18th of May, when Sergei Skripal was discharged from Salisbury District Hospital, since when he has not been seen; plus of course March 4th when it all began.

Within days of the Skripal poisoning, a meeting of British cabinet ministers were *sure of Russian guilt* - and it was the seamlessly-constructed analogy with the earlier Litvinenko affair which generated that consensus.

The Novichok narrative involves *five* people being poisoned by it then recovering: first Sergei and Yulia Skripal, then officer Detective Sgt. Nick Bailey, weeks later Charlie Rowley and then Alexei Navalny. Only one person is alleged to have died of the fabled Novichok namely Dawn Sturgess and even then the Wiltshire coroner was unable to find anyone prepared to put their name on a death certificate stating that she had died of this poison, despite being under enormous political pressure to do so. Successive Dawn Sturgess inquests kept being delayed and finally the whole process was moved to Royal Courts of Justice in London. After more millions have been spent on the year-long hearing (one cannot rush these things), presumably we will at last hear the pre-ordained verdict. The state needs to have at least one person certified as having died of Novichok – otherwise, what was all the fuss about?

Navalny, the Russian Dissident

When, on almost no evidence, Alexei Navalny was alleged to have been poisoned by the same celebrated poison as had been given to the Skripals two years earlier, loud calls for sanctions against Russia were heard, plus renewed demands for the nearly-completed Nord Stream II pipeline to be cancelled. The EU instructed Germany to abandon it! In February of 2021 huge demonstrations were taking place across Russia in support of Navalny, as he was put in jail; while at the same time his anti-Putin video - two hours long - climbed up above one hundred million views. The timing was impeccable. He had spent a couple of weeks in Germany making the film –with an American film company.

Following a massive media blitz on his alleged poisoning - totally presupposing Russian guilt and in defiance of the clear testimony of the emergency-treatment experts at the hospital who saved his life - the European Union Parliament condemned the 'repeated use of chemical nerve agents against Russian citizens,' thereby bracketing the Skripal and Navalny cases together. It called upon Germany to scrap the Nordstream-II project. That was just weeks after the Navalny incident (17.9.20).

It was the Russian medics who performed the only analyses worth anything, at the Omsk hospital where they seem to have saved the life of

Alexei Navalny. They took blood and urine samples right away, not days later as happened in Germany. Despite that it was not able to compare its results with the German labs as they kept pleading to do: that could not happen because the blame and guilt had been pre-ordained - the Novichok story would have swiftly fallen apart had Russian medics been allowed to participate.

For three months international diplomacy had been accusing Russia on the basis that a water bottle in Navalny's hotel room –which he'd supposedly drunk the previous evening – had contained the deadly nerve-toxin, surreptitiously planted by unseen secret agents. No wonder he collapsed on the aeroplane. Then, *four months* after the event, that water bottle faded out of the story and it became Navalny's *blue underpants* which had secretly been contaminated! How could that have happened? These stories are never tried in a court of law, where they would at once fall apart and instead we have trial by media with the sole intention of establishing Russian guilt.

This dramatic 'Novichok Part II' story gained just as much publicity as had the earlier Skripal narrative. In both cases it is doubtful any Novichok was actually used and the 'victims' soon recovered. Two years and a thousand miles apart, both featured categorical accusations against Russia whose guilt was deemed to be, in the words of British Prime Minister Theresa May, 'highly likely.' Woven with great ingenuity, these interlinked stories both made accusations of Russia poisoning its own dissidents and both (I here argue) were achieved *largely by British Intelligence.* Both featured an almost comically inept duo of would-be poisoners incriminating themselves by leaving a trail of their uniquely-distinctive poison all over the place.

If the present narrative can unfold with some confidence, it is because of the work of *three truthseekers* who have endeavored to ascertain the real stories. For each of these three events, the achieving of a truthful narrative has largely depended upon one person! For the Litvinenko affair (2006) we turn to William Dunkerley, whose two poorly-written but insightful books of 2011 and 2015[19] contrast with the well-written but

[19] Dunkerley, *Op. cit.* 2015 and *The Phoney Litvinenko Murder,* 2011.

false-narrative text by Luke Harding, of 2016.[20] The latter has received many glowing reviews, such as 'breathless page-turner,' 'a vital account of the story of the decade and the issue of our age,' etc. For the Skripal story, insofar as clarity has been achieved we need to thank the Salisbury resident Rob Slane, as the thousands of comments on his *Blogmire* articles testify. By interviewing locals he managed to ascertain vital time and space co-ordinates for who did what to whom on the fateful morning of March 4th, 2018. Excellent analyses of the topic have also featured in the *Off-Guardian* and by Craig Murray.[21] For the Navalny story – the West's Trojan Horse to undermine Russia – one is thankful to the persistently-insightful Moscow resident John Helmer, on his 'Dances with Bears' website.[22] The Russian 'Vesti News' channel has made an excellent online video entitled, 'Navalny Fake Poisoning' (24.8.21).

Alexander Litvinenko was probably 44 years old at his death[23] whereas Yulia and Sergei Skripal were 33 and 66 years when allegedly poisoned. Dawn Sturgess died aged 44 years. A couple of years later, Alexei Navalny and his charming side-kick Maria Pevchikh were aged 33 and 44 years when they entered history. State-fabricated terror in the 21st century strangely keeps throwing up such recurring number-patterns, enigmatic and yet plain for all too see.

Are these Freemasonic or Kabbalistic number codes? An appendix to my opus *False flags over Europe A History of State-fabricated terror* (2019) examined the patterns found in these dates, which show *a lot* of 11s, 22s and 77s, eleven being the most frequent prime number involved. As Kevin Barrett commented laconically, 'All those elevens, like those in 9/11, 11/22 and so on, are probably just a coincidence.' Some theorise that the Kennedy assassination on 22nd of November (22/11) was a beginning of this dreadful new *mathesis*.

We're reminded of the British army's cadre of keyboard warriors the 77th Brigade. Located in Berkshire they aim to use 'legitimate non-military levers as a means to adapt behaviors of the opposing forces and

---

[20] Luke Harding, *A Very Expensive Poison, the definitive Story of the Murder of Litvinenko and Russia's war with the West.*

[21] See 'The Miracle of Salisbury' and 'Ten Points I Just Can't Believe About the Official Skripal Narrative' on Craig Murray's blog.

[22] John Helmer's book *Skripal in Prison,* 2020 is a compendium of his essays on the topic.

[23] Born in August 1962 according to *The Independent's* orbituary, though some have given a later date.

adversaries.' Who might they be? On the thesis of this book, their work serves more to create and bolster the image of an adversary than to 'adapt' to it.

The great hope of Vladimir Putin's years of government, of a friendly, post cold-war Europe, whereby the old Iron Curtain would be consigned to history with Europe becoming a continent of lasting peace – that has, in recent years, been extinguished, as threats and baiting insults replaced diplomacy.

MH-17

Compare these two stitched-up 'Novichok' psy-ops to the shootdown of the Malaysian passenger plane MH-17 over the Ukraine a few years earlier (17.7.14), likewise blamed on Russia. Russian satellites had significant telemetry data which could have greatly helped indicate what had happened and it was important for this not to be included in any enquiry. The shootdown event was a Kiev-NATO operation and had emerged from a war-game drill then ongoing (called *Rapid Trident*). An international, Dutch-co-ordinated enquiry from which Russia was excluded at the start was set up not so much to determine what had happened but rather to ratify the pre-ordained Russian guilt. Its purpose was successful, to drum up a new Cold War mentality, to replace and extinguish the old idea of diplomacy. There are intriguing connections here with another Malaysian plane the MH-360 shot down over the Indian Ocean some months earlier. Malaysia had recently held a tribunal which found Israel guilty of war crimes and so maybe Malaysia needed to be taught a lesson. To quote that sage American Paul Craig Roberts,

> The Western media fell in step and blamed the downed Malaysian airliner on Russia. No evidence was provided. In its place the media used constant repetition. Washington withheld the evidence that proved Kiev was responsible. The media's purpose was not to tell the truth, but to demonise Russia.[24]

Or, here is Gordon Duff, editor in chief of *Veterans Today*, which is usually very clued-up on these matters:

> Today, Dutch investigators came up with their long

[24] Blog of 19.8.14, 'In the West respect for truth no longer exists'

> predetermined solution, that a BUK missile shot down MH17 no matter how impossible that might be. Any other answer would have brought down NATO.... Other than the simple issue of impossibility, there is rock-solid evidence that MH-17 was trailed by two SU25 aircraft that Kiev claimed could not be responsible, because they were not capable of flight at that altitude.[25]

That Boeing 777, Flight MH-17, was shot down out of the sky on 17/7. The maiden flight of that Boeing MH-17 had likewise been on 17 July, 1997. Such numbers appear as a signature of state-fabricated terror in this 21st century: for reasons that are obscure.

The MH-17 shootdown had a major influence in destabilising détente as it obliged the nation-states of Europe to endorse a bogus narrative. They didn't have to, but they chose to. There could never be an open enquiry into the MH-17 event: all that could happen – as Russia was obliged to note – was the endorsement of a pre-set Russia-did-it narrative. That is always the case with state-fabricated terror. John Helmer has written a book on the subject which one may compare with a chapter by this author on the subject.[26] For readers not inclined to peruse either of these, Mr Helmer's Amazon page blurb may suffice:

> The first published investigation of the fate of Malaysia Airlines Flight MH17, shot down over Ukraine on July 17, 2014, proving the Dutch Government is running a show trial, with Dutch judges, prosecutors, lawyers, and police serving as soldiers in the Kiev regime and NATO war against Russia. Every one of them is making more money than they were before MH17 was shot down — €35 million more for the judges; €13 million more for the prosecutors; €221 million for the police. An encyclopaedic record of Ukrainian evidence tampering, US satellite photograph faking, and 'witness lying' under Ukrainian Security Service torture and bribery to demonstrate that the Russians accused have no case to answer; that the judge's guilty verdict has been rigged in advance, and that the defence lawyers for the Russian accused should now walk out of the court. Part I, The Dead Talk Back; Part II, Double

---

[25] Duff, *Veterans Today,* 'Media Control and a Rigged report MH17' 13.11.15.

[26] N.K., *False Flags over Europe* (2018) Chapter 10; John Helmer, *The Lie that Shot Down MH-17* (2020).

Dutch; and Part III, The Standard of Proof, unravel the Dutch lying which began, as Chapter 2 reveals for the first time, from the minute the wreckage of the aircraft and the bodies of its 298 occupants hit the ground. Part IV, The Trial, exposes the show in a trial which is too unlawful to be staged in a British or American court.

In such enquiries, whether of the MH-17 shootdown or the poisoning episodes here examined, Russia is not allowed to participate - it is just banned and then blamed!

Following that plane crash on 17th of July, a mere five days later on 22nd of July Theresa May announced that there would indeed be an Enquiry into the Litvinenko affair, and that duly began a week later at the end of the month. There had been years of procrastinating – then the event was finally decided on during an intense blast of anti-Russian sentiment.

In a general sense it would help if an 'awake' politician could be aware that Russia was not actually involved in the Litvinenko, Skripal or Navalny stories (2006, 2018, 2020) in just the same way that Muslims were not involved in the great 'terror' events of this century (9/11, the 7/7 London bombings, etc): even if they have to remain silent after having realised these things. Aye, there's the rub. That will immediately raise the question of, who is doing them? Let's just say this is the 'enemy within,' the traitors within the gates who misuse the public's trust to perpetrate the unmentionable. If indeed state-fabricated terror is the main art-form of this 21st century – as I have averred[27] – then this means that the 'conspiracy theorists' or truth-tellers become the main and in a sense the only real enemy of the state. They have to be continually pulverised. See eg the periodic media-damnations of me (in *the Guardian, Observer, Hate not Hope*, etc).

Truth as such has no meaning within the Empire: an operation is successful or it is not and that is all that counts. It is only credibility that matters, will the people believe it? It is not entirely evident that real passengers died in that plane crash, just as it is far from evident that the crashed plane was the one that was supposed to have taken off at the Schipol airport in Amsterdam that morning: one must regret the absence

[27] NK *Op. Cit.* 2018 p.237.

of interest in discussing such intriguing issues, by people who want to believe what they read in the newspapers.

The Tactics of Deception

A covert operation is one in which what you see is *not* what happened.

British Intelligence has developed a distinctive approach to untruth-fabrication as propaganda for use in war. For the real beginning of this Black Art one needs to go back to the First World War. How were troops persuaded to fight against a nation that had never attacked us in its entire history and only ever desired friendship and which shared the same royal family? That takes quite a skill, one which Britain has got *par excellence* – and can't seem to get rid of:

The indelible memory of atrocity stories that had taken place only

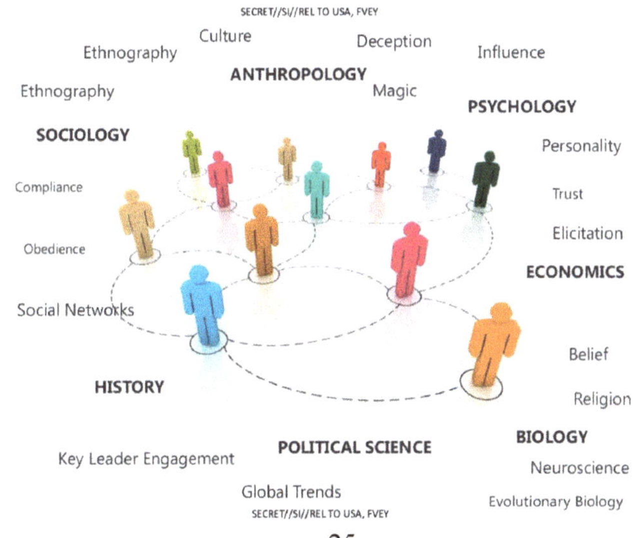

SECRET//SI//REL TO USA, FVEY
10 Principles for Influence
The Time Principle
The Need and Greed Principle
The Deception Principle
The Dishonesty Principle
The Social Compliance/ Authority Principle
The Herd Principle
The Distraction Principle
The Consistency Principle
The Reciprocity Principle
The Flattery Principle
SECRET//SI//REL TO USA, FVEY

in the imaginations of British propaganda agents proved to be stronger and more persistent than any facts. This curious discovery, the power of myths over facts, was the real legacy of the First World War…Britain's propaganda machine, an infernal engine created in war, but impossible to switch off in time of peace.[28]

A dire climax was reached in 2003 when British Intelligence fabricated the bogus Iraq WMD dossier, whereby a pack of lies led to a war that killed some half a million people, after which Tony Blair was re-elected. Was there ever such a group of warmongers as British Intelligence?

Britain's 'Government Centre Head Quarters' (GCHQ) in Cheltenham evidently reckoned a decade ago that some sort of war was being waged, albeit covertly. This we gather from documents released by

GCHQ
NATIONAL SECURITY AGENCY
UNITED STATES OF AMERICA

28 Richard Milton, *The Best of Enemies* 2007 p.68.

SECRET//SI//REL TO USA, FVEY

Gambits for Deception

Attention	Control attention Conspicuity & Expectancies	The big move covers the little move	The Target looks where you look	Attention drops at the perceived end	Repetition reduces vigilance
Perception	Mask/Mimic Eliminate - Blend Recreate - Imitate	Repackage/Invent Modify old cues Create new cues	Dazzle/Decoy Blur old cues Create alternate cues	Make the cue dynamic	Stimulate multiple sensors
Sensemaking	Exploit prior beliefs	Present story fragments	Repetition creates expectancies	Haversack Ruse (The Piece of Bad Luck)	Swap the real for the false, & vice versa
Affect	Create Cognitive Stress	Create Physiological Stress	Create Affective Stress (+/-)	Cialdini+2	Exploit shared affect
Behaviour	Simulate the action	Simulate the outcome	Time-shift perceived behaviour	Divorce behaviour from outcome	Channel behaviour

SECRET//SI//REL TO USA, FVEY

Edward Snowden in 2013[29], entitled *'The Art of Deception: training for a new generation of Online covert Operations,'* marked 'top secret' and 'Only for dissemination within Five Eyes intelligence.' Some of its slides illustrating this fiendish art of deception are here shown.

The 'analysis tools' used by the Joint Threat Research Intelligence Group include the occult-sounding *Shadowcat, Changeling, Poison Arrow, Airwolf, Birdstrike, Angry Pirate* and *Serpents Tongue*. As regards the Dark Web browser 'TOR' neophytes are advised to use '*Astral Projection*: remote SGM secure covert internet proxy using TOR hidden services.'[30] Has GCHQ gone over to the Dark Side? Its 'Psychology of Deception' page includes the skill of 'Mirroring/mimicry' and one would not doubt its effectiveness. Its ten 'Principles of Influence' (see above) include *flattery,*

DISRUPTION
Operational Playbook

- Infiltration Operation
- Ruse Operation
- Set Piece Operation
- False Flag Operation
- False Rescue Operation
- Disruption Operation
- Sting Operation

---

29 'GCHQ JTRIG Tools and Techniques for propaganda and internet deception' 15.7.14; N.B. my terroronthetube.co.uk, p.12, 'Black arts at GCHQ.'

30 The Intercept 'JTRIG Tools and Techniques' 14.7.14. theintercept.com 'The Art of Deception: training for a new generation of online covert operations' 25.2.14

deception and *dishonesty*. Of those ten principles, not one is edifying or honourable. How disgraceful that taxpayers money is being used for such training!

We were left waiting to be told against whom these straight-from-Hell techniques are to be used. Persons who seem on the surface to be politicians and diplomats may actually be trained in these infernal tactics, so wholly devoid of ethical constraint. 'FVEY' as marked on the top and bottom of every slide here alludes to 'Five Eyes', viz. the intel agencies of USA, UK, Canada, Australia and New Zealand, to whom they were presumably sent.

The documents were disclosed by former NSA employee and American whistleblower Edward Snowden in 2013 and included details on GCHQ's close connection with America's NSA, which has endured for 75 years.[31] The latter had been funding GCHQ to the tune of over £100 million over the years 2010 to 2013, by means of which it secured influence over the latter's intelligence-gathering programs.[32]

31 RTNews, 8.3.21 Kit Klarenberg, 'Britain's GCHQ and America's NSA hail 75th anniversary of their alliance.'

32 *The Guardian* 1.8.13 'NSA pays 100m for secret funding for GCHQ Secret payments revealed in links by Edward Snowden, GCHQ expected to 'pull its weight' for Americans'.

PART I

Litvinenko: the Insoluble Enigma

The Skripal Comparison

Discussions of the Skripal story of 2018 have normally alluded to the earlier Litvinenko story of 2006 by way of comparison - thus author and BBC correspondent Mark Urban viewed the Skripal case as echoing the earlier poisoning of Litvinenko: 'for many of those hearing the news, assessing each new fact, trying to understand it all, there was a sort of default setting, the Litvinenko affair.'[33] The latter has been much used in official statements to set up the let's-blame-Russia narrative: as two Russians were accused of having poisoned the 44-year old Alexei Litvinenko, likewise two Russians were accused of having poisoned the 66-year old Sergei Skripal. Thus Wiltshire coroner David Ridley felt there was

> … a remarkable similarity to the belief that the attack on Mr Skripal in March 2018 was carried out by agents of the Russian state on the instruction of the Russian state … The Litvinenko case's similarity with the incident involving Mr Skripal … continues in that a full and detailed criminal investigation revealed two Russian Nationals who were suspected of his murder.[34]

A year later, he explained to a European Court of Human Rights Convention that *by way of analogy* with 'Mr Litvinenko's death in relation to the March 2018 incident here in Salisbury, the CPS confirmed in September 2018 that there was sufficient evidence to make charges of serious homicide criminal offences.'[35] That earlier event more or less enabled the Crown Prosecution Service to point the finger of blame at Russia.

Author William Dunkerley was startled to discover that no certificate

---

[33] Quoted by John Helmer *Skripal In Prison* 2020, p.3

[34] Ibid, p.285.

[35] Ibid, p.284. His 'Ruling' given to the European Court of Human Rights.

had been issued by any Coroner's office as to the cause or manner of his death. Seemingly it had not been settled that Litvinenko's death was a homicide, though he had died from polonium poisoning: he concluded, 'As of October 2011…no certification has been issued as to the cause and manner of death…'[36] That stimulated him to write a couple of books on the subject. The matter was summarised by the perceptive John Helmer:

> There was no inquest in the Litvinenko case. Instead, between his death on November 23, 2006, the opening of an inquest on November 30, followed by five years of adjournments of the inquest, two years of pre-inquest reviews, legal and political argument over a judicial review, and a year and a half of public enquiry, there was a decade of delay.[37]

Litvinenko's father Walter made a comparison with the Skripal case on the *Russia Today* program. In a discussion with Viktoria Skripal, a close relative of the Skripals who lives in Moscow, he explained that originally he did believe the British case, that Russians had poisoned his son. But since then having seen the light he warned her:

> It's not beneficial for them if Skripal stays alive. And this girl [Yulia] – she knows nothing. Skripal knows. She simply came to visit her father and got into this. They'll let his daughter walk away, probably. But if she knows anything, she won't get out of it either.[38]

Alas, how true! He explained how the British government had even denied him access to the files on his son's death, whereby he had not been allowed to see the autopsy report of his own son! The RT interviewer Ms Oksana asked pertinently: 'Doesn't London itself have the capability, intent and motive for this kind of national character-assassination?' Walter was with his son during his last days, following which he made the dreadful accusation against his motherland Russia that its government was guilty. Years later after much heart-searching he changed his mind. He denied that his son was a traitor to Russia which was the alleged motive. He added that 'dozens' of people had been involved, who had made the polonium traces left around! Alexander

---

[36] William Dunkerley, *The Phony Litvinenko Murder* (2011) p.111; see also his *The Litvinenko Murder Case Solved.* (2015)
[37] Helmer, Ibid, p285
[38] *RT interview, 2.8.18 also 1.4.18*

Goldfarb was a 'CIA man' whom, he reckoned, 'killed my son.' As a biochemist and CIA agent Goldfarb was part of the inner circle of Russian tycoon Boris Berezovsky and had visited London at least thrice in the month before Litvinenko's death and met with the victim four times.

Asked about how Theresa May as Home Secretary had 'classified' the Litvinenko documents as being a matter of national security, Walter replied:

> It's now clear why all the documents on the Litvinenko case are highly classified in London for the next 100 years. It was, by the way, carried out by Theresa May. And nobody asked her why on earth she had to classify something that had been on everyone's lips.

Both stories featured an exotic headline-grabbing chemical or element, which was then detected as left behind in all sorts of places. In both cases we are *very* short of credible details as regards how they were detected – as a science historian I am particularly disturbed by this. The two trails – of polonium and then later of Novichok - had provided 'clues' to the police. Traces of polonium were allegedly found in places where the accused persons resided or travelled, eg on their plane back to Moscow. Walter had finally decided not to believe this!

> The FSB [Federal Security Services] wouldn't send some dumbhead to spill polonium on himself, to leave traces all over my son. It appears that someone left traces of polonium on Lugovoy intentionally. Polonium traces were found at the stadium, on the road and even on a plane.

– shades of the the Zizzi restaurant in Salisbury being allegedly contaminated by Novichok! To quote 'antiwar.com',

> If Litvinenko was poisoned, it was the clumsiest assassination in all of recorded history, because the assassins left a radioactive trail that stretched from Germany to Heathrow airport and from there snaked across Europe, contaminating airliners, hotels, private homes, and God knows where else.[39]

[39] 27.11.06 antiwar.com 'the nuking of Alexander Litvinenko'

Litvinenko had a brother Maksim who lived in Italy. In the year 2016, after the verdict of the Enquiry came out, he stated:[40]

> My father and I are sure that the Russian authorities are not involved. It's all a set-up to put pressure on the Russian government.

That was, he reckoned, the reason why the enquiry was only held ten years after the death. In his view,

> The Russians had no reason to want Alexander dead. My brother was not a spy, he was more like a policeman...he was in the FSB [Russian Federal Security Service] but he worked against organized crime, murders, arms trafficking, stuff like that. I believe he could have been killed by another poison, maybe thallium, which killed him slowly, and the polonium was planted afterwards. Now after 10 years any trace [of polonium] would have disappeared anyway, so we will never know.

That does make a lot of sense. He found it odd that requests to have his brother's body exhumed, in order to verify the presence of polonium, were denied by Britain - even the request to release Litvinenko's body to the family was refused! Such British hanky-panky has to be the reason why British authorities refused to collaborate with Russian investigators on the case and that again forms a major point of comparison with the Skripal story. These remarks by Maksim Litvinenko came in response to the appearance of sir Robert Owen's official report on the Litvinenko death.

It is remarkable that both the brother and father were 'sure' that Russian authorities were not involved.

Some years later in 2021 the Parliament of the European Union passed a motion accusing Russia of the Litvinenko poisoning. It reiterated- to anticipate ahead somewhat – the daft teapot story, according to which Lugovoy sprinkled some of the polonium isotope into a teapot in a busy Mayfair hotel (Sometimes one feels that MI5 is hard-pressed to come up with decent stories). Thereby the cluster of three false narratives – Litvinenko, Skripal and Navalny – remain together, temporally conjoined, to be invoked in the minds of the NATO-warmonger

[40] 22.1.16 'Britain had more motivation to kill Aleksandr Litvinenko than Russia, brother claims' RT News.

politicians, for their successful purpose of re-establishing their new Cold War. Except that his time, it may not remain so cold.

In July of 2014 the Home Office announced that at long last there would be a public enquiry into the 2006 Litvinenko death. Prime Minister David Cameron used this moment to set up sanctions against Russia, because he could also invoke the MH17 'airliner atrocity' of that same month with its presumed Russian guilt (Why would Russia cause a Dutch passenger plane to crash in Ukraine?). He urged a 'moment of action' against Russia and called for sanctions, 'the hardest since the Cold war.' (30.7.14 *The Independent*) This was three years before Britain's next Prime Minster Theresa May was to declare Russia an official enemy – maybe *the* enemy, as China had not then quite grown to its present co-enemy status. *Homo exterminans* works through such fictional, illusory narratives which are designed to create hate and fear, in order to maintain the *everlasting-war* condition, to prevent peace from breaking out and stop anyone from ever having a thought about what it might mean to be human. *The people have to live in fear* – that is the fundamental political principle of this 21st century. Prime Minister Cameron came out with the vile accusation that Russia was guilty of 'State-sponsored murder' – this on the basis of a highly conjectural Enquiry-cum-murder trial at which no defence lawyers were present. Détente is thereby destroyed with the largest country on earth and to what aim?

The previous year, Britain's Foreign Secretary William Hague had successfully argued that information pertaining to the Litvinenko case should be kept secret as being 'a risk to National Security' and what was that all about? Initially there was going to be an Inquest, then, to quote sir Robert Owen, 'the inquest was replaced by the Public Inquiry:' there never was an Inquest though this is supposed to happen following a controversial death. An inquest would have obliged named experts to appear in public and say how exactly they ascertained the extraordinary cause of death, allegedly one tenth of a microgram of polonium-210 in the body(*The Times*, 18th December); and to do so preferably within a year of the death not ten years later. An Inquest is not allowed to cast blame for the death but only examine its cause: as the whole point was to blame Russia, an Enquiry was required not an Inquest!

Polonium

'A Very Expensive poison' was the title of *Guardian* journalist Luke Harding's book, his allegedly 'definitive story' of the case. It had no references or bibliography and was basically a 'gripping yarn'. He averred that the polonium used would have cost 'tens of millions of dollars'[41] and moreover had to have come from a specific Russian nuclear power plant, implying that it therefore had to be a state-sponsored event: 'Avangard became the only place in the world where one particular isotope was made.'[42] This was despite a claim in the *New York Times* that a lethal dose could cost a mere $22[43] - quoting a Princeton physicist saying 'You can get it all over the place.'

The director of the Russian Federal Atomic Energy Agency Sergei Kiriyenko stated that Russia had made no exports of polonium to Britain in the past five years. "Allegations that someone stole it during production are absolutely unfounded... The controls are very tough."[44]

The Palestinian leader Yasser Arafat seems to have been killed by the polonium-210 isotope two years earlier in 2004. His body was exhumed some years later and high levels of the isotope were found.[45] If so it would have to be a state-sponsored event as that element is one of the world's rarest and most tightly controlled radioactive isotopes, used in nuclear weapons. The following laconic comment from Israel Shamir, made in the context of the Alexei Navalny 'Novichok' story, compares the narratives:

> Why wait for the medical reports when the story has already been written? The poison libel is well established. A KGB renegade Litvinenko was poisoned by Polonium-210 and expired painfully in London. Who shall we blame? Putin. (Yasser Arafat, the Palestinian leader, had been poisoned by the same radioactive material at the same time, and it was suggested that Israelis are behind it, but such details would just confuse the reader). A retired

[41] Harding, p.337.
[42] Luke Harding, *A Very Expensive Poison*, p.171.
[43] NY Times 3.12.06, Polonium, "By some estimates, a lethal dose might cost as little as $22.50, plus tax"
[44] Ibid.
[45] 'Tests carried out by the *Institut de Radiophysique* (Inst. of Radiation Physics) at the U. of Lausanne in Switzerland found traces of polonium, a rare, highly radioactive element, on Arafat's personal belongings' (wiki).

spy, Mr Skripal (who allegedly authored the Steele Dossier with its pissing prostitutes that almost derailed Trump's presidency) was supposedly poisoned by the military-grade nerve poison, Novichok. It happened in vicinity of Porton Down, the British chemical warfare centre, but don't let it confuse you. Let's blame Putin.

He quickly recovered but that was just further proof (as if we need any!) that Putin and his intelligence community love non-lethal poisoning with intricate poison.[46]

If the polonium had come from Israel as a component of its covert nuclear program then that would indeed explain the paranoid air of secrecy which has hung over the entire British Government narrative. Arafat died on November 11th 2004, then two years later around November 11th it became evident that Litvinenko had been poisoned and was dying: 'on 11 November, a week after he was admitted, something terrible and strange happened. Litvinenko's hair started to fall out.'[47] Twelve days later he was dead.

The UK Atomic Weapons Establishment at Aldermaston in Berkshire examined Litvinenko's urine. It suspended a silver disc in it, and polonium adheres to the metal surface. Thereby we're told they could obtain traces of it, enough to analyse its radiation-signature. From its alpha-ray emissions they could supposedly tell that it was polonium. That was reported in *the Guardian, ten years* after the event (16.1.16). This sounds like impressive gee-whiz British science, (or perhaps, Mediaeval alchemy) however it was strangely unreported at the time. I scoured newspapers plus also science journals – *Science, Nature,* the *New Scientist, Journal of Toxicology* – published around the end of 2006 but found nothing.[48] If that was how it was detected, how, we may wonder, would much lower levels of polonium have been detected on airplane seats? Those of us who bothered to get a science degree would have appreciated some slight details here and not just from a journalist, to bolster the credibility of the narrative.

---

[46] Unz.com Israel Shamir, 'Navalny Poison' 1.9.20

[47] Harding, p.140.

[48] Harrison, Ghent and Black 'the Evidence for the use of Polonium-210 to poison Mr Litvinenko, Joint Experts Report' (Public Health England) was prepared for the Inquest, so maybe in 2012: NRO LITV-2-DJK-1.

The day after the death 24th of November Scotland Yard was saying they were 'treating it as an unexplained death' and medical experts at UCH the hospital concerned were saying that a battery of tests had ruled out radiation poisoning. Was it, maybe, a chemotherapy drug, they wondered? (*The Times* 24.11.06)

The Accused

Six months after the mystery death in November of 2006, the police announced that they had a murder suspect, namely Andrey Lugovoy. No court or inquest had ascertained that it was a murder - as opposed to accidental contamination - or that it was the radioactive isotope polonium-210 that had killed him. Lugovoy, then a wealthy businessman and politician in Moscow who ran a private security firm, had formerly been a KGB agent. Later he came to sit in the Russian parliament, being elected in 2007 as a member for the 'far-right' Liberal Democratic Party of Russia.

At the time (November-December 2006) he was working for the exiled oligarch Boris Berezovsky in a capacity of providing security. The latter had long been an arch-enemy of Vladimir Putin, so is it likely that Lugovoy would then be operating on instructions from Moscow to do such a deed? In his statement of innocence[49] he said: 'the British security services could have been involved. I don't want to say that they had masterminded that murder, though anything can be expected from these guys ... Litvinenko definitely worked in the interests of intelligence and counter-intelligence services.' 'Since Litvinenko was a British spy' he followed somebody's instructions in compliance with the rules and discipline existing in the organization he worked for: 'So it means that the British secret services were somewhere near and could be linked to Litvinenko's death.'[50] Lugovoy was thus accusing the British secret services of being linked to the death. He continued:

> Then how did it happen that all the places in London where we met with Litvinenko only in October, but not in November, were marked, I want to stress the word 'marked', by polonium, and why was polonium found aboard the planes on which Dima and I came

---

[49] rt.com/news/andrey-lugovoy-calls-himself-victim-in-litvinenko-case - his statement of innocence plus Q&A.

[50] https://www.rt.com/news/andrey-lugovoy-calls-himself-victim-in-litvinenko-case/

> back to Moscow and Germany respectively, back in October 2006? I have only one conclusion: we were marked by polonium on purpose for further use in the political scandal… it is not a secret any longer that all my contacts with Litvinenko were under tight control of the British special services.

He described how the latter was a kind of friend, within the circle of London Russian-dissidents, but that he had not liked it when Litvinenko had tried to recruit him as an anti-Putin 'agent':

> I got an opinion that he was obviously getting out of the British special services' control. I think the unsuccessful attempt to recruit me considerably undermined his significance with the British. Trying to fulfil the intelligence officers' task at any price, Litvinenko often exceeded the role of a recruiting agent and let out too much information while talking to me. For example, the British did not like him for boasting to have contacts with high-rank officials of MI6. Therefore, it is hard to forget that Litvinenko became another out-of-control agent of the British secret Service and they got rid of him, if not the Service itself, then under its control and with its connivance.

He wondered as to what motive he was supposed to have had for the deed - was he some kind of

> Russian James Bond, who can infiltrate into a nuclear research laboratory as well as cold-bloodily poison his buddy, incidentally contaminating his children, his wife, his friends and himself as well? All this performed in a one-man show of the terrorist Lugovoy, incidentally losing his business and clients. And the most important question –for what reason? Where is my motive?
>
> I am convinced that polonium was used to mark us and the places which we attended. I draw your attention to the fact that polonium was found only a month after we left Britain. On November 1 my wife and three children were with me and nobody was planning to meet Litvinenko, but he called us many times and asked to meet him precisely in the hotel.

Let us compare this view with that of French special-ops Intel officer

Paul Barill given in 2016. [51] His comments in the Q & A session here quoted could just be the *only* correct assessment of the whole murky business:

"Now it is necessary to reveal the truth – so many lies were told by journalists, but above all by the secret services. I especially want to make this clear – for America and Britain, the cold war still continues, and in the Litvinenko case we're talking about an operation to destabilise the Russian leadership, to seriously damage the reputation and credibility of the internal security forces. This manipulation operation is co-ordinated by the CIA and MI6 and all enemies of Russia.

I am a resident of London, I know London, in London live about three hundred thousand Russians. All Putin's opponent are in London.

Q So who killed him and why?

"He received two different doses of polonium. One of them has not really been investigated: I'm talking about the trail of Scaramella, who met Litvinenko in the morning and dined with him in Piccadilly. The first traces of Po were in the restaurant where they had dinner together. Scaramella then went to Italy where he was arrested upon arrival… But all this was building up, as all this was controlled by the master who was pulling the strings, in whose hands was concentrated all the information that was to be used against Russia and President Putin. It was Mr Berezovsky.

Q But ultimately, for whom did Mr Litvinenko work?

"Litvinenko was an ex-agent of the FSB…Berezovsky harboured a growing hatred for President Putin. Berezovsky began to gather together all the opposition who were in London. They repeatedly visited him, who paid them for information. Mr Browder was closely connected with Berezovsk, and Mr Litvinenko was in his service, and did everything asked of him by Berezovsky.

Berezovsk collaborated with Browder, an American agent, to blacken Putin's image. They carried out manipulation and destabilisation

[51] 'EXCLUSIVE: French Spec Ops Captain Paul Barril Reveals How Litvinenko Was Killed' 13.4.16; discussed by Dunkerley, 'A US-UK Plot to Discredit Putin and Destabilize the Russian Federation' on wikispooks.com, 31.3.16.

actions, eg Browder disseminated the rumours that Putin had 200 billion dollars which he keeps outside of Russia, and that's false. All activities were co-ordinated by the two.

Q Who actually killed A Litvinenko?

"First of all he was closely connected with the Chechen mafia. At the core of all conflicts among the London opposition were financial conflicts. Litvinenko received substantial sums from Berezovsky, who was to pass them onto the Chechen group who carried out targeted operations. He was not supposed to know everything. Polonium was delivered from Russia through a Chechen-Italian connection, through Scaramella who held a warehouse of Russian arms in Naples. What business could he have in Naples? It was purely financial manipulation, but the main overall goal was to shake the position of President Putin and weaken FSB.

Q So Litvinenko was executed by Chechens and Scaramella?

"He was eliminated, he became a stone around his [Berezovsky's] neck and began to disturb him... Litvinenko was an agent of MI6, under constant guard by Scotland Yard. They gave him freedom of action. His affairs were directed against President Putin.

Q So Litvinenko invited Lugovoy to come?

"Yes he asked him to come because he wanted to get information from him. He was the bearer of information. Litvinenko was supposed to pay Lugovoy. Mr Scaramella, he slipped polonium in the tea before ..he was involved in the delivery of the polonium, chosen specifically because it was a brand of Russian production and hence to implicate the FGB. So it was Scaramella. He killed Litvinenko. But who slipped the polonium? People was circulated from hand to hand, people did not know its dangers.

The judge who conducted the investigation determined that there were no traces of polonium on the plane, on which the Russian flew, and no traces at the airport where the Russian arrived."

On the allegedly-fateful day of November 1st Litvinenko's first meeting had been with Scaramella in the early afternoon at a 'Sushi bar' in Piccadilly after which he went onto the 'Millennium' Mayfair suite at around 3 pm. Scaramella had some list he wanted to discuss but 'before the pair could discuss the list further he [Litvinenko] complained of feeling violently unwell.' (21.11.06 *The Times*)

Litvinenko had been working as a journalist for a Chechen newspaper, the nearest thing he had to a career. He had never been a Russian spy, contrary to so many newspaper headlines. Both he and Lugovoy were then in the pay of the Russian billionaire Berezovsky.

Litvinenko was contaminated in the weeks prior to November 1st as shown in the docu-film "The Case of Alexander Litvinenko - Through Sherlock's Eyes'.[52] This was narrated by the Russian 'Sherlock Holmes' actor Vasily Livanov (MBE). It features the genial owner Dave West of the Abracadabra bar in Jermyn Street explaining that Litvinenko had been visiting his club a full week before the supposed poisoning, but *not* after, and that various polonium traces had been detected around his club. Neither Brerezovsky nor Lukovoi had ever visited it to his knowledge. He would have given this as evidence to the Enquiry had he not alas been murdered in December 2014, shortly before the film emerged.

If we turn to the book by *Guardian* correspondent Luke Harding, he describes the two alleged assassins Lugovoy and Kovtun visiting this Russian Abracadabra bar – which he claims is a bordello – in the week before November 1st, and not accompanied by Litvinenko.[53] Readers may wish to view the film online and judge for themselves which of these two versions is correct. The police did, the film tells us, definitely find polonium traces in the club. These two different accounts have very different implications.

The film's producer Alexander Korobko, the CEO of 'Russian Hour' was asked the ultimate 'Who did it?' question and replied, '"I think it was a sales operation that went wrong. Litvinenko was known to be careless, he'd play with his gun in his pocket... and they were not careful with this substance" implying that it was accidental self-poisoning.

The film also features Lugovoi taking a Polygraph lie-detector test in 2012, which he passed; plus evidence from a former White House radiological advisor on the availability of Polonium 210.

---

[52] Hosted by *Russia Insider* on facebook.com entitled, "Bombshell video: Vital Litvinenko Murder Clues Unearthed by Amateur Sherlock Fans."

[53] *A Very Expensive Poison, the Definitive Story of the Murder of Litvinenko,* 2016, p.93.

Nuclear Smuggling and Blackmail

Four days after the death of Litvinenko *The Independent* revealed that he had been involved in the smuggling of nuclear material: "Alexander Litvinenko, the poisoned former Russian agent, told the Italian academic he met on the day he fell ill that he had organized the smuggling of nuclear material out of Russia for his security service employers." (29.11.06) He had admitted to Scaramella that he had "masterminded the smuggling of radioactive material to Zurich in 2000," thus -

> The European media is now reporting that Litvinenko was involved in smuggling nuclear materials from Russia to Zurich in 2000 and that he may have continued his involvement in nuclear smuggling. Some reports, including recent comments to the BBC by Litvinenko's friend, Italian "security expert" Mario Scaramella, suggest that Litvinenko was involved in the smuggling on radioactive materials. An accident involved in the smuggling of nuclear materials may have resulted in Litvinenko's poisoning from radioactive polonium-210. Litvinenko's involvement with the Chechen Mujaheddin, said to be allied with the so-called "Al Qaeda," his links to the same European organized crime smuggling networks that were the subject of surveillance by outed CIA agent Valerie Plame Wilson and her Brewster Jennings & Associates covert CIA front company, and his links to Israel-based Russian gangsters all add to a mounting pile of evidence of "Al Qaeda" links to the Russian-Israeli Mafia. The Chechen press release reference to "the weapon" may have been hinting at a project to build a radioactive "dirty bomb" by Litvinenko. London's *Observer* surmised as much in a December 3 report: "Among the theories that remain open is that the poisonings were an accident that happened while Litvinenko tried to assemble a dirty bomb for Chechen rebels. Those who know him believe he was crazy enough to attempt such a thing and, in the past week, some have implicated him in the smuggling of nuclear materials from Russia." (AntiWar.com[54])

Litvinenko had co-authored a book with Yuri Felshtinsky. The latter

[54] original.antiwar.com 'Litvinenko: Blackmailer, Smuggler, Gangster Extraordinaire' 4.12.06

appeared in *The Charlie Rose Show* on American TV on December 5th a week after his colleague had passed away and stated: 'We were talking probably fifteen or twenty minutes by phone, probably on 8th November, and at that time Litvinenko was sure that it was Mario Scaramella who poisoned him.'[55]

It is quite feasible that Litvinenko was involved in nuclear smuggling, with his extensive underworld connections. To quote again from Antiwar.com,[56] 'That he wound up being contaminated by the goods he was peddling on the black market seems far more credible than the cock-and-bull story about a vast Russian plot originating in the Kremlin.' One colleague of his said: 'He met so many real criminals. He understood really bad people, how bad they are. And yet he was very optimistic.'[57] That is a perilous space to occupy, as an exile in a foreign country.

Mario Scaramella from Naples had a deep knowledge of nuclear materials and was present at that November 1st tea party. He did not eat or drink anything, then came down with a mild case of polonium poisoning afterwards.[58] He was arrested on his return to Naples. The two of them seem to have had links to the same European organized crime smuggling networks[59] and Scaramella was suspected of arms trafficking, having been convicted in Italy for selling arms. The public prosecutor of Naples has attempted to investigate this offense but was obliged to desist: his view was that Scaramella was in close relationship and maybe working for, the CIA.

Polonium 210 is one of the three ingredients needed to build a clandestine nuclear bomb. In Israel, Litvinenko met Leonid Nevzlin the CEO of the company Yukos, shortly before he died. Some surmise that Israel was the source of the radioactive material. Traces of it were found at Berezovsky's residence and on the British Airway planes Litvinenko was on, to and from Israel.

In the months before his death Litvinenko seems to have been talking about blackmailing people. Evidence for this was provided at the

---

[55] Dunkerley, 2011 op.cit., p.22.

[56] Antiwar.com, 'the Craziest conspiracy of them all' 22.1.16.

[57] Judgement made by fellow exile Viktor Suvorov: Harding op.cit, p.19.

[58] Wiki, 'Mario Scaramella'

59 For view of French Intel officer Paul Barill, search for 'Litvinenko, Berezovky, Skripal ... CIA, MI6 False flags to blame Russia' 15.3.18 (video deleted)

Enquiry by Dr. Yulia Svetlichnaya, a postgraduate student at Westminster University, who interviewed Litvinenko six times before his death. During these meetings he would harp on about the blackmail he was going to carry out, she recalled. Lugovoy's Statement of Innocence also remarked upon this. Litvinenko's previous work as a policeman might have given him knowledge about various people he might try to blackmail. An in-depth critique of the Enquiry's Report on the Saker website commented:

> Though Dr. Svetlichnaya's evidence has been known about since just after Litvinenko's death, her evidence has been largely ignored, with some casting doubt on the truth of it. The Inquiry report shows that Dr. Svetlichnaya was closely questioned by the Inquiry, and it is clear from the report that she came through the cross-examination well. The Judge never casts doubt on her truthfulness, and there is no reason to doubt therefore that her story is true.
>
> We know therefore that in the months leading up to his death Litvinenko was talking about blackmailing someone. Unlike the nebulous claims of motive that have been made against the Russian authorities, blackmail is a classic motive for murder.[60]

Figure: Mr Berezovsky

As regards income, he was being paid £2000 a month as an MI6 agent- as his widow disclosed[61] - plus he was a regular correspondent for the Chechen Press State News Agency, then also he was being looked after by the Russian Jewish billionaire Berezovsky, becoming in effect 'Berezovsky's security advisor.' The latter had been paying for the

[60] russia-insider.com/ 'The Litvinenko Inquiry: London's absurd show trial' 26.1.16

[61] *Daily Mail*, October 2007.

education of Litvinenko's son to attend private school, and, as the BBC reported, owned the house that Litvinenko was living in.[62] That sounds like a perilous lifestyle - especially for one regarded as a 'walking encyclopaedia of organized crime.'[63]. Quite a lot of people might have wanted to do him in.

If there was one person who really knew what had happened to Litvinenko, was Berezovsky. He was the spider at the centre of a web of Russian anti-Kremlin dissidents in London and seems to have been at one point plotting an overthrow of the Russian government. Various people around him met premature ends then he himself 'committed suicide' in 2012. William Dunkerley in his ambitiously-entitled book *Litvinenko Murder Case solved* stated, "the finger of suspicion points to persons who were born in Russia, but are now closely connected with London...The entire Western news story about Putin being behind the murder of Litvinenko was fabricated apparently by the Berezovsky camp...' Thus, it was a close associate of Berezovsky Alexander Goldfarb who claimed that Litvinenko had made a 'deathbed confession' dictated to him, which received a lot of publicity, whereas it later transpired he had written it.[64] Litvinenko, whose English was very poor, had only signed it as he lay dying.

After losing a multimillion-pound lawsuit against a fellow-billionaire, Berezovsky received the following ethical damnation from the judge:

> I found Mr. Berezovsky an unimpressive, and inherently unreliable, witness, who regarded truth as a transitory, flexible concept, which could be moulded to suit his current purposes. At times, the evidence which he gave was deliberately dishonest; sometimes he was clearly making his evidence up as he went along...[65]

Only after his visit to the dying Litvinenko on November 19th did there began the nonstop flow of Russia-did-it newspaper stories: should we really be trusting a narrative having such a source?

---

[62] Dunkerley, *The Phony Litvinenko Murder*, p.67.
[63] Harding pp.5, 48.
[64] Dunkerely, 2015, pp. 110-11, 119.
[65] High Court of Justice, 31.8.12 Berezovsky Vs Abramovich, section 100.

The Teapot of Death

I am sure that Mr Lugovoi and Mr Kovtun placed the polonium 210 in the teapot at the Pine Bar on 1 November 2006. Judge Owen at the 2012 Inquest

The polonium-in-teapot story at the Mayfair hotel only surfaced *three months* after the death, on 26 January 2007, even though allegedly discovered early in December. This allegedly-radioactive teapot was giving 'off-the-chart' readings for polonium, the Inquest was told ten years later.[66] People wondered how the continued use of such a contaminated teapot could have created no risk to public health as was averred: members of the public who had subsequently had tea from that teapot, how come they were unharmed? Others wondered how the dose was strong enough to leave such a high reading after six weeks of cleaning and re-use, while weak enough to take three weeks to kill Litvinenko.

A detailed account of the contamination found in that Millennium Bar had appeared in a *Panorama* programme just days before the teapot story appeared and made no mention of it, which some found rather odd. Earlier a tea cup used in the Pine Bar in Soho had been found to be contaminated, on 9th of December. The teapot story itself took a bit longer to materialise, following which the police reckoned they had enough evidence to issue an arrest warrant for Andrei Lugovoi.

On the afternoon of November 1st, Lugovoy had agreed to meet Litvinenko in the Mayfair hotel tea-room. He brought his wife and children because, he explained, they had been on their way to watch a football-match. He and another friend who was also there enjoyed a few drinks to fortify themselves, but Litvinenko who never touched alcohol merely had a sip of tea. The notion that in such a situation Lugovoy would take out a phial of deadly, radioactive polonium and pour it into the teapot seems laughably absurd. Would it not have been seen by all sorts of people in that crowded bar? And was not Litvinenko himself sitting right there? On his recollection it was Litvinenko who had phoned him up and invited him for afternoon tea, however the British story has it the other way round.[67]

---

[66] The Independent 28.1.07 'The Poisoned Teapot'
[67] Luke Harding, *A Very Expensive Poison*, op.cit., p.129.

Figure: Andrei Lugovoi, Deputy of the State Duma, the lower House of the Russian parliament

If indeed Lugovoy was taking his family to watch a football match that afternoon – as has not been disputed - the idea that he would have proposed a meeting with Litvinenko on that same afternoon seems unlikely, on which basis one might tend to concur with his version of events, that it was Litvinenko who phoned him, wanting the meeting on that day.

The official narrative had the poison uniquely affecting Litvinenko - but why did not half the kitchen staff get infected at the hotel upon washing up the tea-pot? It's arguably the most deadly poison there is, being highly radioactive (its half-life is a mere 140 days). A similar problem was later raised in the Skripal and Navalny stories, that somehow the poison had been applied very specifically such that unintended victims were not affected.

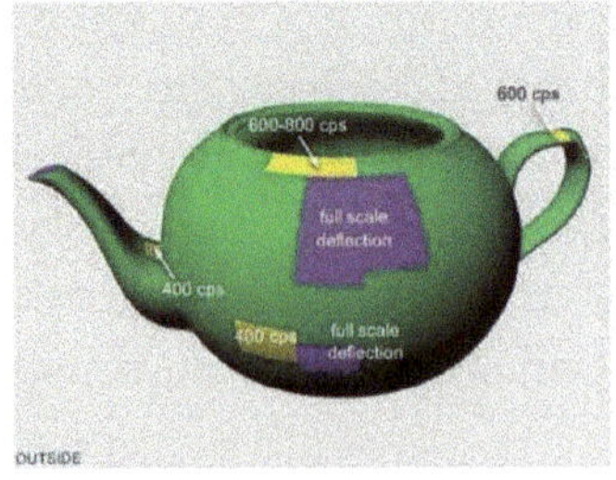

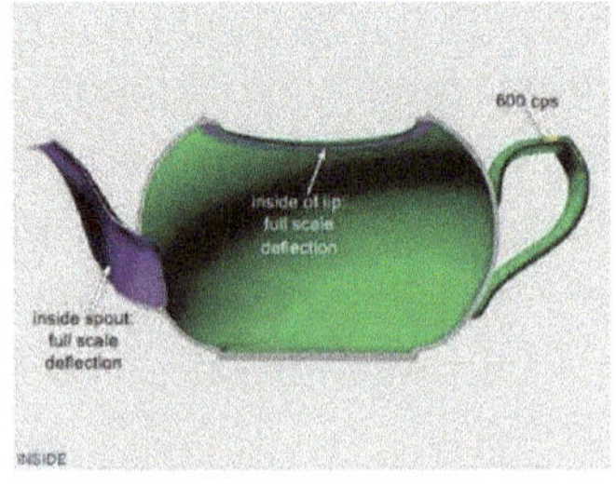

Figure: High teapot radioactivity readings, as given to the Litvinenko Enquiry

CCTV footage or witness testimony, supporting the claim that Litvinenko was poisoned in the Pine Bar, has never appeared – a sure indication of State activity. Ditto for the Skripal narrative, where bloggers kept asking, where is the CCTV?

The Secretive Enquiry

William Dunkerley was asked in 2012 as to why the Litvinenko investigation had been dragging on so long and replied, 'That's perhaps more a mystery than Litvinenko's death.'[68] Britain's Home Secretary in that year Theresa May declared that an Enquiry into the murky case would be 'against the national interest,' but finally in 2014 a High Court ruling came out saying that, yes, there had to be one! What, we may wonder, was the big secret? In the end a rather non-public enquiry took place, presided over by retired High Court judge Sir Robert Owen. Conducted mainly in secret, closed hearings, it heard testimony given by anonymous witnesses and evidence 'assessed as being too sensitive to put into the public domain.'

Sir Robert's Report concluded 'I have no evidence at all that either Mr Lugovoy or Mr Kovtun had any personal reason to kill Mr Litvinenko.'[69] Those were his concluding words! But that did not hinder him from accusing the two Russians of murder - Russian guilt was, after all, 'strongly suspected.' The two accused, Andrei Lugovoi and Kovtun, were denied sight of much of the evidence and had therefore refused to take part. Sir Robert Owen commented at length in his judgment about this refusal but omitted to state the reason for it.

The Report confirmed the truth of what the US journalist William Dunkerley had always said about Litvinenko's famous death-bed statement, that it did not originate with him but was put together by others who got him – as he lay dying – to sign it.[70]

The Judge conceded that Lugovoi's behaviour at the Pine Bar of the Millennium Hotel was hardly consistent with his being the poisoner: he showed indifference to whether Litvinenko drank the poisoned tea or not and had also introduced to Litvinenko his young son, which he would surely not have done had he thought there was danger to his son from the polonium.

---

[68] Dunkerely, *Litvinenko Murder case Solved* 2015 p.98.

[69] politico.eu "Putin 'probably approved' Litvinenko murder" 21.1.16; gov.uk, 'The Litvinenko Inquiry' 9.2.

[70] Inquiry op.cit., 3.145

As regards the notion that the FSB had sought to recruit Lugovoi, his closest and most visible connections since the 1990s had not been with them but with the Russian oligarch Boris Berezovsky - whose relations with the FSB were already very bad, even when he had been a major figure in Russian politics in the 1990s. The Judge conceded that Berezovsky continued to think of Lugovoi as his friend right up to the moment when Litvinenko was killed. Lugovoy is unlikely to have been an FSB agent.

Here is Dunkerley again with the Skripal analogy:

> It sounds like the same old story again that was put forth about the polonium and Litvinenko's case, where people said it was from Russia and it could be traced back to a specific place, although there were subsequent expert testimonies that that was in fact not even possible
>
> Certainly there are differences between the two cases, but there's one thing that is almost exactly the same: it is that both cases are based on hearsay information and lack factual bases. In that regard they're the same.
>
> The Litvinenko case, as far as the public description of what happened, was a hoax in my view. There was no factual basis, the coroner's inquest didn't start until around five years after his death and before the inquest opened, the British prosecutor Ken Macdonald had said that he had grave suspicions there was Russian state involvement - grave suspicions is a long way from having a case, so I don't think that anything that transpired with Robert Owen's inquest or inquiry has any legitimacy. He was definitely on a witch hunt looking for Russian state involvement.[71]

Here's an Italian view[72]:

> During his military service in Chechnya he had contacts with the local mafia, then one of the most dangerous brotherhoods.. Litvinenko belonged to the world of English espionage, where lies and fantasy intermingle without being able to discern at what point one begins and the other ends…

---

[71] Dunkerley, SputnikNews.com 20.3.18

[72] "The dark Litvinenko case" by Rodolfo Bueno for Rebelión. http://www.rebelion.org/noticia.php?id=208303

> Despite he never met Lugovoi or Kovtun, because they appeared on the scene later for allegedly poisoning Litvinenko with polonium 210, Scaramella also was poisoned with the radioactive substance, which he discovered upon arrival in Italy soon after.
>
> The real criminal is the one that takes greater advantage of the crime, that is the law of Sherlock Holmes, and it is the globalized world imperialism which exploits the fuss that is made of the death of Litvinenko,…
>
> Even Litvinenko's father says that in England he was offered the moon and the stars to testify that Putin was behind the murder of his son.

The Saker column - always worth consulting on Russian affairs - commented on the Enquiry:

> Despite twisting the evidence and throwing legal procedure out of the window it failed to show the Russian authorities killed Litvinenko. It could only say "probably" – an absurd verdict the evidence contradicts.
>
> But the purpose of the inquiry was never to establish the objective facts, separate the guilty from the innocent, or discover the deeper causes and motives behind events. As far as 21st century imperialist propagandists are concerned, these are quaint and even amusing concepts. The point is to catapult a lie into as many headlines as possible, so that by the time the truth emerges the damage has already been done.[73]

Initially Russians had asked to participate in the enquiry, after all was it not a Russian who had died? A senior Russian diplomat stated: 'It is in the Kremlin's interest to offer full co-operation with the British police in trying to find the would-be assassin. This was not some official hit as so much of the British press would have it, so let us investigate this thoroughly wherever it takes us. The finger has been pointed at us so let us find who was truly responsible.' (22.11.06 *The Times*) However that could not be allowed - Russia was after all to blame. Complicated webs

---

[73] https://thesaker.is/the-litvinenko-inquiry-londons-absurd-show-trial/ Saker essay Alexander Mercouris (practicing lawyer for 12 years at the Royal courts of Justice) copied from *Russia Insider*.

of British duplicity means that we'll never get to the answer. Years later another international scandal was to blow up with a claim that another Russian, Alexei Navalny, had been poisoned again via a cup of tea, a story which turned out to be just as unverifiable and where once again Russia was excluded from the investigation.

'I don't know' is the hardest thing to say. Seven million pounds were reportedly spent upon the Enquiry, and yet its single-minded focus upon Russian guilt rather prevented examination of other more probable explanations nearer to home.

Four Russian diplomats were expelled after the Litvinenko death – compared with the twenty-three expelled twelve years later over the Skripal affair.

> O what a tangled web we weave
> When first we practice to deceive
>
> Sir Walter Scott

Part II: WHAT HAPPENED TO THE SKRIPALS?

The Skripal-Novichok Timeline, 2018

20 Feb UK army's three-week Operation Toxic Dagger on Salisbury Plain, CBW simulation

2 March US TV shows *Strike Back: Retribution* series with a Russian Novichok-poison conspiracy

3 March Julia Skripal arrives at Heathrow from Russia

4 March The Skripals fall unconscious

5 March *Clinical Services Jnl.* says Skripals poisoned by Fentanyl

12 March May names Novichok + 'highly likely' Russia did it.

13 March May phones Trump over Dead Ducks story.

14 March UK expels Russian diplomats

15 March G7 summit accuses Russia of poisoning,

16 March Letter from Salisbury hospital doctor in *The Times*

18 March Police contact parents of child at duckpond

22 March OPCW allowed to take Skripal blood samples

24 March Yulia emerges from coma.
Novichok is alleged on Skripal's door-handle.

26 March Expulsion of Russian diplomats from US and EU

9 April Yulia leaves hospital, goes to Fairford RAF Airbase.

14 April US & UK bomb Damascus

18 April Sergei discharged from hospital.
Salisbury official denies 'dead ducks' story.

4 May Police visit City Stay Hotel in Bow, samples taken.

23 May Yulia's one post-Event media appearance

27 June Charlie Rowley says he finds bottle in a bin.

30 June Charlie Rowley and Dawn Sturgess found unconscious

4 July Rowley & Sturgess in critical condition
Neil Basu: the couple were poisoned with Novichok

8 July Dawn Sturgess dies

11 July Small bottle found in Rowley's home with Novichok

24 July Yulia phones her grandmother

8 August US announces sanctions against Russia

5 Sept Traces of Novichok found in City Stay Hotel.

5 Sept Two Russian suspects named, Petrov & Boshirov.

Novichok in Storyland

In the late autumn of 2017, a Sky-TV thriller series called *Strike Back: Retribution* began. It wove a tale of international intrigue involving an imaginary nerve poison called 'Novichok'. Thus, for example, in Episode 4 'General Lázsló shuts down Section 20, forcing Donovan to work in secret. She discovers that Zaryn is in fact Karim Markov, a Russian scientist who allegedly killed his colleagues with Novichok, a nerve agent they invented,' etc. In the film it was a 'binary' weapon, i.e. the toxin was made by mixing two compounds together. The timing *synchronised with* the real-life event:

Episode 4

November 21, 2017 (UK) and Feb. 23, 2018 (US)

Episode 5

November 28, 2017 (UK) and March 2, 2018 (US)

Episode 6

January 31, 2018 (UK) and March 9, 2018 (US)

(reference here is wiki/Strike Back: Retribution)

The Empire has to tell us what it plans to do in advance, or so we're told: it's called 'Predictive programming.' As Webster Tarpley wrote in 2005: "No terrorist attack would be complete without the advance airing of a scenario docudrama to provide the population with a conceptual scheme to help them understand the coming events in the sense intended by the oligarchy" (*Synthetic Terror*, p.408). Supposedly it obtains our tacit agreement by informing us in advance, or that's the theory.

It's strange that a British-American intelligence TV drama Strike Back had several episodes featuring Novichok nerve agent and Evil Russkies last year. Someone orchestrating political theater in the UK watches a lot of TV, or is advised by its producers. en.wikipedia.org/wiki/Strike_Ba...

8:32 PM - Mar 15, 2018

Whether or not the Skripal event was pre-planned, that ongoing TV series helped to create the script. It was a source of ideas, for those seeking an anti-Russian angle. Britain's Conservative government was greatly failing in its Brexit negotiations and needed some distraction, plus the British intervention in Syria was increasingly being exposed as *pro-terrorist,* whereby the deceptive 'White Helmets' were faking alleged Syrian government chemical attacks on the Syrian people.[74] British jets had been bombing Syrian cities for quite a long time, and why were they doing that? There was a perceived danger, that the Russian forces who had been invited into Syria by the legitimate government and who were fighting against ISIL or al-Qaeda, i.e. against the terrorists, would be perceived as being the good guys, a legitimate force in the area. The timely insertion of a counter-narrative was necessary.

Russia's chemical weapon stockpiles were finally destroyed in the autumn of 2017, and the Director-General of the OPCW stated[75]:

> The completion of the verified destruction of Russia's chemical weapons programme is a major milestone in the achievement of the goals of the Chemical Weapons Convention. I congratulate Russia and I commend all of their experts who were involved for their professionalism and dedication. I also express my appreciation to the States Parties that assisted the Russian Federation with its destruction program and thank the OPCW staff who verified the destruction.

It was on the 11th of October, 2017, in the margins of the 86th Session of the Executive Council of the Organisation for the Prohibition of Chemical Weapons (OPCW), that a ceremony was held to mark the completion of the destruction of the Russian Federation's chemical weapons.

Meanwhile, the British chemical weapons laboratory Porton Down had received over the last decade some seventy million dollars from the Pentagon for research and development, for *further developing* nerve

---

74 See eg *Veterans Today*; 'Swedish Medical Associations Says White Helmets Murdered Kids for Fake Gas Attack Videos' 6.4.17 Gordon Duff (although NB The Swedish Doctors for Human rights did express some scruples about this VT account).

75 opcw.org 27.9.17, 'OPCW Director-General Commends Major Milestone as Russia Completes Destruction of Chemical Weapons Stockpile under OPCW Verification.' See also SIPRI Yearbook for 2018, reporting on how Russia 'completed destruction of its stockpile in 2017' (p.348).

agents and other chemical weapons. They were tested on lab animals, with over a hundred thousand being 'used' for the Pentagon project. The effect of sulphur, mustard and also phosgene gas on the lungs of various animals was investigated. In this way the Pentagon gained access to Porton Down's scientific and technical capabilities along with other test data. The US army continues to produce deadly viruses, bacteria and toxins in violation of the UN Convention on the Prohibition of Biological Weapons.[76]

So, while Russia was fully complying with the destruction of its chemical weapons stockpiles, in a transparent and verifiable manner, the US and UK had been conducting what the convention defines as forbidden research, using live lab-animals.[77] That perspective may help us to appreciate the depth of mendacity involved in the Skripal story - which took place a mere six miles from the Porton Down laboratories.

A month before the event, Britain's Defence Secretary Gavin Williamson had been raving to *The Telegraph* about the dire threat posed by Russians: they were going to cause 'so much pain to Britain,'[78] he explained, and had been spying on Britain's infrastructure in order to see how they could 'damage its economy, rip its infrastructure apart, actually cause thousands and thousands and thousands of deaths,' etc. But no-one believed him: even for *Daily Telegraph* readers, this was too much. Could an event therefore be arranged, to alert Britons to this danger?

For three weeks prior to the event the British army war-gamed 'Operation Toxic Dagger' on Salisbury plain simulating a chemical warfare attack, over February-March 2018:

> The three-week exercise included company-level attacks and various CBRN (chemical, biological, radioactive and nuclear) scenarios based on the latest threats for ultimate realism, such as a raid on a suspected chemical weapons lab. It climaxes with a full-scale exercise involving government and industry scientists and

76 'The US Army regularly produces deadly viruses, bacteria and toxins in direct violation of the UN Convention on the prohibition of Biological Weapons:' *WMD America: Inside the Pentagon's Global Bioweapons Industry*, '21st Century Wire,' 21.1.18.

77 'Salisbury attack reveals $70 million Pentagon program at Porton Down' By Dilyana Gaytandzhieva 30.4.18

78 Globalresearch.ca 'UK Defence Secretary Accuses Russia of Planning to Kill "Thousands and Thousands and Thousands" of Britons,' 28.1.18

> more than 300 military personnel ... casualty treatment was a key part of the Salisbury Plain exercise. A chemical decontamination area was set up not merely to treat 'polluted' commandos, but also any wounded prisoners they may have brought in; once cleansed, casualties can be treated in field/regular hospitals...[79]

State-fabricated terror normally features such a drill, conducted and timed with the event or just before it.[80] The plans that mature during the drill, then *result in* the event itself.

The Trump 'Dirty Dossier'

As a double-agent who had betrayed his Russian colleagues, Sergei Skripal was jailed and then released on a spy-swap. He had ostensibly been living quietly in Salisbury since then, but it seems that he had actually been helping with 'Orbis Business Intelligence' run by a rather shady ex-MI6 agent called Christopher Steele. The Democrat party in America had requested that he help them before the US election in brewing up dirt on Trump. They paid Steele to do this, assuming that Hilary Clinton would win and that such foul play would never see the light of day. But it did all emerge and the *New Yorker* called Steele 'the man behind the Trump dossier.'[81]

Andrew Wood, a former British ambassador to Moscow, was employed by the 'Institute for Statecraft', and he passed on the Steele dossier_to U.S. Senator John McCain, who gave it to FBI Director James Comey. The FBI first used the dossier to get federal warrants to spy on the Trump campaign, and after Comey was fired to launch a counter-intelligence investigation against Trump himself. Thereby an all-British pack of lies seems to have more or less paralysed the US government for a couple of years.

This 'dirty dossier' not only alleged Russian interference in US elections but also contained the so-called 'golden showers' document,

---

79 Nuclear-news.net 'The Skripals and the unusual timing of chemical warfare exercises near Salisbury.' 6.4.18.

80 NK, *False Flags over Europe,* 2018.

81 New Yorker 12.3.18 'Steele the Man Behind the Trump dossier'

weaving a tale about Trump being in collusion with Putin if not a Russian agent. A "failed spy" had relied upon "made-up facts by sleazebag political operatives" as President Trump rightly observed.[82] As regards its influence, one must agree that:

> … the very dirty and obviously fake dossier on Donald Trump and Vladimir Putin has sustained the Russiagate scandal for almost two years in the United States, throwing this country into a McCarthyite hysteria..[83]

It formed 'the insane underpinning of the whole mad Mueller probe into "Russian collusion"'[84] (Robert Mueller was a former FBI Director). For two years the US Department of Justice conducted an enquiry, into whether the US President was a Russian agent, where the *only evidence* for its treasonous claim was the Steele dossier. Even as late as February 2019 former FBI director Andrew McCabe was wondering on national TV if America's President is a Russian agent. Can a nation be governed under such circumstances? There is real evidence for interference in the 2016 US elections, however they were interfered with by the UK – not Russia.

In November of 2018 a UK 'Anonymous' collective started releasing tranches of documents on 'Integrity Initiative,' which derived from the 'Institute of Statecraft.' To quote again from the US Lyndon Larouche website, it comprised:

> … an international network of politicians, journalists, academics, foundations, and military officers engaged in a very dirty black propaganda campaign funded by the British Foreign and Commonwealth Office, NATO, Facebook, and such intelligence quangos as the Smith Richardson Foundation here in the United States, all while posing as a Scottish charity.

Funded by the UK government, it swiftly became apparent that its meaning was very much the opposite of integrity or statecraft: in a secret and mendacious manner it was generating anti-Russian propaganda. We

82 Ibid.
83 Larouchepac.com 'the British role in the Coup against the President is now exposed.' 10.1.19 See Appendix.
84 Michael Anthony, 'The Alternative Skripal Narrative' on *The Saker* website, 17.2.19.

may quote again from the US Larouche foundation (See Appendix), as to how British lies were being spread across Europe:

> This methodology, fully implemented in the British propaganda and regime change operation against Putin, which began with the Litvinenko poisoning in 2006 and dramatically escalated in 2014, has created an astounding and deranged war fever against Putin in Britain and throughout Europe...
>
> The Institute has recently opened major operations targeting Germany, seeking to smear and defame existing German networks urging peace with Russia while attempting to build the same war fever they have created in Washington and London.[85]

Key names appear in this shadowy organization: Christopher Steele, Mark Urban - the BBC political correspondent who started writing his book on the Skripal affair in 2017 a year *before* it had happened - and Pablo Miller OBE, a longtime 'handler' of Skripal. We may surmise that the latter moved to Salisbury after his release from Russia because Miller lived there. Miller was then working for Steele, his old boss at MI6, in the private intelligence firm *Orbis*.

Names connected with the White Helmets in Syria also link to the Institute of Statecraft. The White Helmets 'charity' claims to be rescuing kids from Syrian government attacks, whereas it has actually been fabricating the mock chemical-weapons attack dramas. These have been used to ratify the US/UK city bombing of Syria.[86]

Sergei Skripal's help would have been needed in preparing the Steele dossier, to give an authentic-sounding Russian Intel angle. In the view of Craig Murray, the Dossier had been written by a Russian "trained in the KGB tradition." After the whole thing backfired with Trump's unexpected electoral victory, followed by the publication of this 'dirty dossier,' it was gratifying to see those responsible in the hot seat.

Following this debacle, the notion of returning to his motherland might have assumed greater urgency for Sergei Skripal. Would he not rapidly become a disposable asset? MI6 would surely assume that he

---

85 Ibid, ref. 27.

86 Vanessa Beezley, 21st Century Wire, 24.2.19: 'WHITE HELMETS: Organ Traffickers, Propagandists… or 'Saints''?

would be discussing that option with his daughter as soon as she arrived. He would not want to go the same way as Litvinenko.

He was a British spy, though the news reports would allude to him as a 'former Russian spy.'

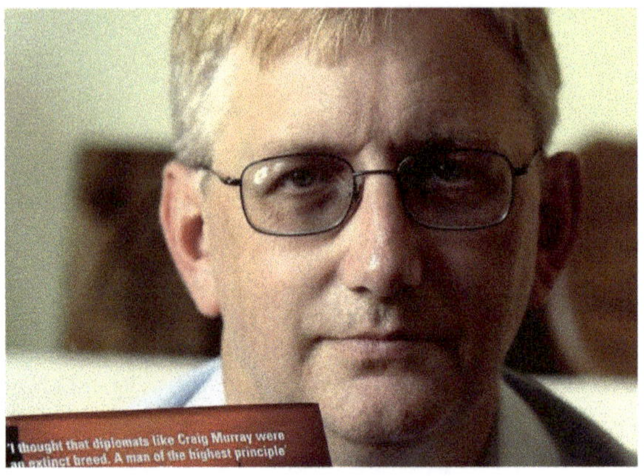

'I thought that diplomats like Craig Murray were
extinct breed. A man of the highest principle'

Craig Murray: a reliable source. His article 'Skripals – the Mystery Deepens' received three thousand comments.

Yulia pays a visit

On March 3rd, Yulia Skripal flew over to Salisbury from Moscow to visit her Father. Sergei Skripal's old friend Ross Cassidy, a construction worker, drove him over to Heathrow airport to pick her up. Mr Cassidy then noticed that Skripal seemed rather jumpy: 'Something had spooked Sergei in the weeks prior to the attack. He was twitchy, I don't know why, and he even changed his mobile phone.'[87] Mr Skripal had by no means fully retired from his life as a double-agent after his release from a Moscow jail in 2010; it is not hard to understand how he might be in such a state.

The day before, two Russians had flown over to visit Salisbury, and then flew back late at night on March 4th the day after. It seems that three seats were booked on that return flight, not two – one which was not

87 Ross Cassidy recalled this six months later in September as we'll see, but I'm suggesting it may be reliable.

used,[88] prompting speculation, as to whether Sergei Skripal was meant to return to Russia on that flight? There would have been every reason for him to wish to return, as he had relatives living over there. If he were then to tell what he knew, might that not somewhat strain the US-UK 'special relationship'? It would have diffused the war-propaganda building up and enabled Trump and Putin to talk to each other. But, for those very reasons, it could not be allowed! Yulia had to put these options to him in person because no phone could be trusted.

The story given by the two Russians – as tourists visiting Salisbury cathedral – was not generally viewed as being very plausible, and the notion that they had come to deliver something seemed to make more sense. As their itinerary around Salisbury brought them quite close to the Skripals on the afternoon of March 4th , people wondered whether there could have been for example a fake passport and air ticket which they somehow delivered to Sergei? Arriving by train into Salisbury station at 11.48 am, they returned later that day and we'll see how the police obfuscated that return time, as if they had jumped on the 1.50 pm train returning to London.[89] Why would they have wanted to do that?

On the morning of March 4th the father and daughter were said to have driven to the local cemetery where Mr Skripal's late wife and son were buried; maybe wanting a quiet spot to talk where they could not be overheard, and maybe to say a final goodbye if Sergei believed he was returning to Russia. Whatever they did, his mobile phone was totally switched off for four hours on that morning. Here is a possible timeline for events of that day:

* At 9:15am on 4 March Mr Skripal seen driving his car. They visit the Salisbury cemetery to pay respects to his dead wife.

* Two Russians allegedly arrive at Skripal door around 12-1 pm. Did Skripals return home around 1 pm & touch the doorknob?

* At 1:30 Mr Skripal's car was seen going towards the town centre.

88 Disclosed in February 2019 by 'Bellingcat,' see M. Anthony 'The Skripal Case, an Alternative narrative' March 2019, off-Guardian.

89 Luke Harding, *The Guardian* 5.9.18 'Planes, trains and fake names: the trail left by Skripal suspects'

* At c. 1.45 they are feeding the ducks.
* At 2 pm they dine at the Zizzi Restaurant.
* At 3 – 3.30 they go to Bishops Mill Pub in the town centre.
* At 4.03 they are 'slumped' on a park bench.
* At 4.10 Alison McCourt and daughter treat them
* At 4.16 first report to the police.
* At 4.27 police check Skripal's wallet & driving licence.
* At 4.40 Air Ambulance helicopter lands in Salisbury
* At 5.00 police car arrives at Skripal home
* At 5.15 the two are taken to Salisbury hospital.

AA Wiltshire Air Ambulance helicopter landed in Salisbury car park and may possibly have airlifted Yulia to hospital.[90] No-one could have identified the couple slumped on the bench until after 4.27 when Skripal's personal belongings were examined. Then a mere twelve minutes later the air-ambulance landed in the middle of Salisbury: which some have viewed as far too short a time-interval, pointing to a pre-set agenda. Ditto for the police car arriving at their home at 5 pm and parking there.

The Zizzi restaurant, where the two had lunch

90 Yulia was admitted to Salisbury Hospital with Patient Admission Number PTN/18/0010 while her father's was PTN/18/0012. The numbers here are not sequential, indicating that some other patient was admitted after Yulia and before Sergei.

Mark Urban in his book tells how the couple walk from the Zizzi's restaurant towards the Maltings (where the park bench was) with some bread to feed the ducks, but then they have to sit down, they feel groggy, sweat profusely, et cetera.[91] That didn't happen!

In contrast, we turn to Rob Slane, a well-informed Salisbury local (whose website *the Blogmire* is the best on the subject), who finds that 'there exists really clear footage of the couple feeding ducks next to the Avon playground' around 1.45 pm., which would be before lunch. He has also stated 'I have had it personally confirmed to me that they were in the pub between 15.00 and 15.30 – after lunch!' There are many CCTV cameras in The Mill pub, and as usual in such cases we're not shown any of it. Here is one local witness he cites:

> Sergei Skripal went for a drink with his daughter at 3pm at The Mill in Salisbury after eating at a Zizzi Italian restaurant. In the pub, they ordered two glasses of wine before Mr Skripal went to use the toilet. The witness, who did not want to be named, …[92]

It seems that the authorities wished to obfuscate the actual sequence, whereby after emerging from their house around or just after 1 pm, they drove off in their car, parked it in town, fed some ducks, went to have lunch in Zizzi's, went to have a drink at *The Mill,* and then strolled over through the shopping centre to The Maltings. This all sounds as if they were enjoying life and not as if they had both received a deadly poison. The picture shown of them in the pub together (see Chapter 11) looks cheerful enough.

Food poisoning at Zizzi's?

Were the two poisoned while they had lunch at the Zizzi restaurant? That was the initial story, however, the image of Russian agents creeping into that crowded, elegant restaurant in the town centre and surreptitiously adding a deadly poison to the food never made any sense, not least because no-one else in the restaurant was affected. The two had enjoyed a meal of risotto pesce with king prawns, mussels and squid

91 M.Urban., *The Skripal Files*, p.213.
92 Theblogmire.com '10 main holes in the official narrative.' August 2018.

rings in a tomato, chilli and white wine sauce. Subsequently the restaurant was closed down and staff uniforms worn on that day were burned (11th March). Even that theatrical act could not make the story appear credible.

A week later, around the 17th of March, police were murmuring that the Novichok had perhaps arrived in Yulia's suitcase, brought over from Moscow – implying that she herself had packed the poison, or at least knew it was there (*The Sun* 18 March 'Russian Plot'). Before that, the police had located it on the car door-handle, but neither of these stories seemed very credible. Finally the locus of the alleged deadly poison had to move again, and *three weeks after the event* it finally ended up located on the Skripal's home door handle (March 24th).

It was raining that day, and the 'gel' – if ever it had existed – would have been water-soluble.

Although the police claim to have CCTV records of Mr Skripal's car driving around Salisbury on that day, they have been strangely vague about whether the Skripals returned to their home at around noon, with different timelines being put out, retired and changed. Supposedly he must have shut his front door upon leaving, and thus became contaminated. Then he held his daughter's hand or arm thereby contaminating her, after which they drove around. They enjoyed lunch in a restaurant and a drink in a pub, then strolled down the central shopping arcade, coming into the park where a light drizzle was falling. The 66-year old man and his 33-year daughter collapsed simultaneously on a park bench, from a toxin received *three hours* earlier, remaining on that bench for an hour then being taken to hospital – with not a single photograph taken. Once again there are problems of credibility here.

Did the two of them suffer food poisoning from the restaurant, as argued by 'Moon of Alabama' on the *Sputnik* RT program? That would indeed give us a pleasantly simple view of events:

> I believe that the Skripals suffered from simple food poisoning. They ate a Risotto Pesce with mussels at the Zizzi restaurant and unintentionally poisoned themselves with Saxitoxin, a natural 'nerve agent' that is also known as shellfish poison.

He went on to explain how British government officials then lifted the Novichok explanation from the *Strike Back* program:

> A day later the government woke up to that fact that the Skripal case could be used to divert from May's problems with the Brexit negotiations and help in upcoming elections. They needed something splashy, to blame it on Russia. Someone in the Government's spin-master group came up with 'Novichok'.[93]

On this view, what 'Moon of Alabama' calls 'the Government's spin-master group' had to act quickly, and were inspired by the *Strike-Back* TV series. Here is the BBC's report, of how the couple were treated:

> A doctor who was one of the first people at the scene has described how she found Ms Skripal slumped unconscious on a bench, vomiting and fitting. She had also lost control of her bodily functions. The woman, who asked not to be named, told the BBC she moved Ms Skripal into the recovery position and opened her airway, as others tended to her father. She said she treated her for almost 30 minutes, saying there was no sign of any chemical agent on Ms Skripal's face or body. The doctor said she had been worried she would be affected by the nerve agent, but added that she "feels fine". (8th March)

This 'high-security' couple in Salisbury, who would be being closely monitored, are suddenly vomiting on a park bench. The nurse (revealed to be Colonel Alison McCourt, a year later) remained unaffected by any symptoms of nerve poisoning.

Porton Down, Britain's main 'Bio-Hazard' research centre, is located a mere six miles away from Salisbury town centre. Immediately after the alleged collapse of the couple, we learnt that, 'The pair are currently in intensive care at Salisbury Hospital under supervision of experts from Public Health England's Centre for Radiation, Chemical and Environmental Hazards.' That was in The *Mirror* on March 6th. In other words, experts from Porton Down were looking after them, and why should that be? We the public were not told of any nerve-poison until the next day, the 7th of March. But experts from Porton Down were immediately present in the hospital, looking after the couple.

93 11.4.18 Sputniknews.com, 'How TV Spy Fiction Helped Sell the Salisbury Poisoning'

A Nurse passing by

The startling identity of the 'off-duty Nurse' who was the first to arrive at the park bench - she just happened to be passing by – only emerged a year later: she turned out to be none other than 'Colonel Alison McCourt,' the army's most senior nurse! She and her daughter both 'treated' the Skripals for which her daughter received an award. She was skilled in dealing with chemical weapons injuries. She stated in a TV interview that 'the woman [Yulia Skripal] was not breathing at the time we found her,' which did not match her initial story. Alison McCourt must have known what was going on, and so the fact that she allowed her daughter to treat the couple indicates that no nerve agent was present.

The Skripals were taken to hospital, and then the next day's medical report had them treated for the drug Fentanyl. The *UK Clinical Services Journal* website reported that the couple were treated for Fentanyl poisoning in Salisbury hospital over the first day March 5th , although that statement was deleted some weeks later.[94] Fentanyl has a reputation as a 'date-rape' drug because it makes people feel sleepy and flop about, unlike a nerve-poison. As a synthetic 'opioid' it can be a recreational drug. Salisbury District Hospital declared a 'major incident' after 'two patients were exposed to an opioid.'

Then on March 7th we heard about Detective Superintendent Nick Bailey, as being in hospital in a coma and 'fighting for his life.' The next day it was revealed that he had arrived at the park bench at around 4.30 pm, and 'caught' the nerve agent. Then after that on the 9th the story changed, and he had visited the Skripals house where he had been poisoned (This was revealed by former London police chief Sir Ian Blair). Upon release from hospital, Nick Bailey said that his experience had

94 The article was up over 26-7th April, but then the Bulgarian journalist Dilyana Gaytandzhieva published this on her social media account, after which its text was changed from 'the drug Fentanyl' to 'a substance.' The online *Clinical Services Journal* article of March 5th 'Response Unit Called As Salisbury Hospital Declares "Major Incident"' alludes merely to 'what is believed to be an opioid.'

had been "completely surreal" and added, "normal life for me will probably never be the same" – doubtless the effect of a Fentanyl coma.

The #Skripals were allegedly exposed to the drug #Fentanyl, not the #Novichok nerve agent, according to information obtained from the UK Clinical Services Journal
clinicalservicesjournal.com/story/25262/re...
10:24 PM - Apr 26, 2018

He then lost his job with the police, lost his allegedly-contaminated home, furniture and car ('We lost everything') and is claiming to be suffering severe, ongoing trauma such that he cannot work with the police force any more![95] Altogether nearly a hundred Wiltshire police officers and staff have needed and received therapy (17.5.18 *The Guardian*): surely a consequence of dealing with a narrative that was incoherent, untrue and in every sense poisonous.

Colonel Alison McCourt: just passing by?

So two quite senior people, one from the police and the other the British Army, happened to be passing by and 'helped' the Skripals.

How did a Detective Superintendent come to be just walking by? How had he been poisoned when the nurse and her daughter who earlier

95 In May 2021 he was suing Wiltshire police in the High Court of Justice for a £1 - £2 million sum. His grounds for doing this remain unclear.

treated the couple were OK? Clive Ponting, an old civil-service whistle-blower, reckoned that: 'the policeman who 'just happened' to be around was almost certainly the special branch "minder" who was keeping Yulia under surveillance.'[96] One could say much the same for the nurse, Colonel Alison McCourt.

A Premeditated Event?

Was the whole event premeditated? Mark Urban OBE, the Diplomatic and defence editor for the BBC, had been an officer in Britain's Royal Tank Regiment together with Pablo Miller – Sergei Skripal's handler. Mr Urban *had already been interviewing* Sergei Skripal for a book the previous year prior to the event, which seemed rather strange. When the story broke and he was the go-to person on the matter, no-one mentioned this! This curious fact only emerged in July of 2018, a few months before his book came out: people wondered how much he had been told by British intelligence on this matter. Had he for example discussed the Trump dossier in his meetings with Pablo Miller and Skripal? He never gave straight answers to these questions. But, when I heard him speak on LBC radio – as a main government spokesperson on the topic - he was articulate and very convincing.

The Government slapped not one but two D-notices upon any mention of Pablo Miller, within a week after the event. He was Skripal's MI6 handler and they used to meet up at least once a month. As Craig Murray surmised, "That the government's very first act on the poisoning was to ban all media mention of Pablo Miller makes it extremely probable that this whole incident is related to the Trump dossier and that Skripal had worked on it."

Let us suppose that the double-agent Skripal wanted to return to Russia, because his mother and son had both died, buried in the Salisbury graveyard, whereas his grandmother was still alive in Russia as was his daughter Yulia. Russia might have accepted such a deal if there was a

96 Craig Murray blog 28.4.19 'Probable Western Responsibility for Skripal poisoning'

About the only decisive public move by the authorities has been to censor MSM via a D Notice last week from fully identifying Mr Skripal's MI6 handler living nearby...

9:14 am - 12 Mar 2018

prospect of him spilling the beans about the alleged Russian interference in the US elections, cooked up by MI6.

Both Skripals seem to have had their mobile phones switched off over four hours on that cold, Sunday morning[97] – or, were their phones only closed off to British intelligence? If such a plan existed, then MI6 would be suspecting and anticipating it – after all, who can say when a double agent is going to turn again?

Sergei Skripal had seemed stressed, agitated and in a hurry to leave Zizzi's restaurant, as the staff there recalled. Could it be that he had an appointment at the park with someone, maybe with one of the two Russian visitors, or even with his handler Pablo Miller? MI6 may have been uneasy about his phone being blocked from them for several hours.

Clearly, someone would have had to give the drug to both of them *before* they collapsed on the park bench. Some witnesses have described the two as being catatonic and immobile as if severely drugged, though I'm doubtful about these.[98] No-one has come up with any credible suggestion as to how such a drug could have been administered, to both of them. Could some Fentanyl-like substance have been administered to them in the ambulance on their way to the hospital?

Fentanyl was also reported in a local news site *Devon Live* on the next day, March 5th:

> It is understood that police suspect fentanyl, a synthetic opiate many times stronger than heroin, may have been involved. A man and a woman are in a critical condition and up to 10 other people are involved.

---

97 Craig Murray 6.9.18 'Skripals: The Mystery Deepens' (NB, this gained three thousand comments!)

98 e.g., Freya Church and Destiny Reynolds.

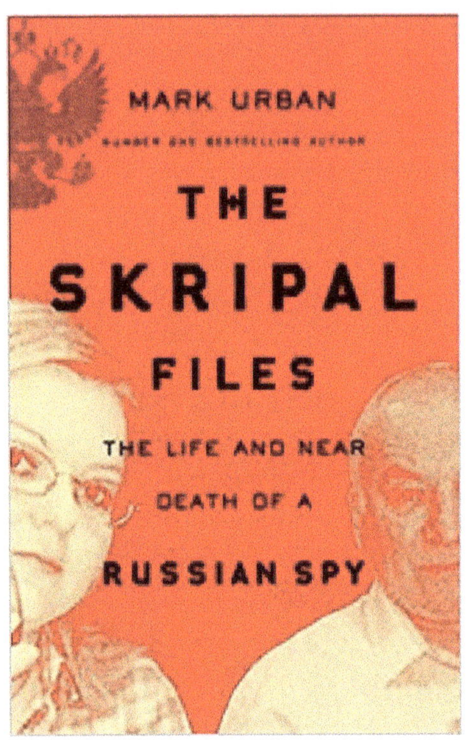

Officers and paramedics were called to The Maltings shopping centre in Salisbury after the man and a woman fell ill. The woman, who was unconscious, was airlifted to Salisbury district hospital at about 4.15pm, while the man was taken by ambulance.

(article called, 'Major chemical incident declared after ten people vomited fentanyl and two are critically ill.')

The 'Wiltshire Air Ambulance' did indeed land at 4.53 pm in Sainsbury's car park, remaining there for ten minutes before taking off - but we lack any account of who got in or out of it. Again this looks very much like part of a pre-arranged narrative, within the 'Operation Toxic Dagger.' Considering that the hospital is a mere two miles from the park bench, an air helicopter lift is never going to make very much sense.

Months later, Mr Skripal's friend Ross Cassidy, a haulage contractor, recalled that the Skripals had been at home that day until after 1 pm – as one might expect for a father and daughter just reunited.[99] Ross Cassidy commented on the location of their home:

> It would have been far too brazen for them [alluding to the two alleged perpetrators] to have walked down a dead end cul-de-sac in broad daylight on a Sunday lunchtime … Sergei's house faces up the cul-de-sac. He had a converted garage that he used as his office – this gives a full view of the street… Almost always, Sergei used to open the door to us before we had a chance to knock.

99 9th September *Daily Mail*, 'Speaking for the first time.'

Figure: Mr Ross Cassidy

From his office, Sergei could look down the little street and see anyone coming: doubtless why MI6 chose that house for him, when he moved to Salisbury.

Ross Cassidy tried to visit the Skripals in hospital, but was denied access. Ditto for a team from *Russia Today* television, they arrived at the Salisbury hospital but were denied access to the Skripals. *Nobody* was allowed – no friends, no relatives. With headlines around the world and diplomats being expelled, it was strange to have no testimony. But, the BBC's correspondent Mark Urban gathered that Ross Cassidy was allowed to visit after Yulia had regained consciousness towards the end of March. She was discharged 9th of April.

Russia is Accused

Thirty senior cabinet ministers gathered together in Whitehall on the morning of Wednesday March 7th, maybe in the underground COBRA office,[100] and these included the Home Secretary Amber Rudd and Foreign Secretary Boris Johnson. On the previous day the word 'Novichok' had started to be used – and yet, noted Mark Urban of this group:

> None of them harboured any doubt that Russia was responsible for what had happened in Salisbury.[101]

If we assume he was correct - and he seems well-informed – we ought surely to enquire, as to the source of such an extraordinary collective certainty, given the complete absence of evidence pointing in any such direction. Psychologists might wish to ponder how such collectively-

100 Cabinet Office Briefing Room A.
101 *The Skripal Files*, p.234.

shared certainty is achieved in the absence of any relevant evidence: could it be some spell, whereby the Reds-under-the-beds paranoia that used to exist several generations ago had been reactivated?

On March 12th, a week after the event, Britain's Prime Minister Theresa May first hurled the dreadful accusation at Russia: a 'military-grade nerve agent of a type developed by Russia' had been used. A couple of days earlier, documents had been produced by the *Integrity Initiative* casting blame on Russia[102], which presumably influenced the Prime Minister. These documents lacked any trace of evidence for Russian guilt and their case *solely depended* upon establishing common ground with the Litvinenko affair twelve years earlier.

Concerning this accusation, Craig Murray commented:

> The "novichok" group of nerve agents will almost certainly have been analysed and reproduced by Porton Down. That is entirely what Porton Down is there for [and] Porton Down has acknowledged in publications it has never seen any Russian "novichoks"... The UK government has absolutely no "fingerprint" information such as impurities that can safely attribute this substance to Russia.... There has in fact never been any evidence that any "novichok" ever existed in Russia itself.[103]

What was this deadly agent, more or less hitherto unknown, which the media were assuring us was more deadly than strychnine? Chemical-weapons experts were seen looking for it, in full protective gear. It was not on any official list of banned nerve agents – as Dr Trapp, a former Secretary of OPCW, declared:[104]

> OPCW does not hold any information on Novichok... Novichoks have indeed not been declared as part of a CW stockpile or past CW production programme by any state party.

Or as Nafeez Ahmed wrote on his blog, 'both Porton Down's Dr. Black and the OPCW's Science Advisory Board fundamentally questioned the "existence" of Novichok'. Russia's Foreign Ministry spokeswoman, Maria Zakharova, clarified this matter:

---

102 syriapropagandamedia.org/working-papers/briefing-note-on-the-integrity-initiative 'Documents related to the Salisbury poisonings'

103 13th March, 'Russian to Judgement'

104 27 March, Nafeez Ahmed blog.

> Never on the territory of the USSR in Soviet times or in the times of the Russian Federation on its territory have there been studies conducted under the code name Novichok. It was neither patented, nor used as a symbol or a code. Once more, as this is the key thing: the word Novichok has never been used in the USSR or in Russia as something related to chemical weapons research. This word was introduced and used for poisonous materials in the West.[105]

The UK refused to comply with Russia's request for a sample of the alleged "novichok" and blocked their resolution at the UN calling for a "co-operative international investigation in line with OPCW standards" (15th March). Was not the UN set up for this very purpose, viz. resolving international tensions by informed debate? All through this brazenly fabricated tale, we find a *complete absence of supporting evidence*: as if the mere word of the UK government should be enough, for the media and UK allies to accept their ever-changing narrative.

The Skripal blood samples arrived at Porton Down for analysis at 6 pm on 5th March, however the MOD has admitted (in response to a FOI request) that it lacks information about when the samples were taken at Salisbury Hospital: it has no proper chain of custody record. Such a broken chain of custody does allow for the possibility that the samples were tampered with and such samples would never be allowed in a court of law.[106]

Theresa May did not allow the OPCW to become involved in the Salisbury event, until a couple of weeks had gone by – by which time anything could have been done to the samples. The director-general of OPCW Jose Bustani wondered, 'Why didn't they call immediately the OPCW? ... They could have done this beforehand, before accusing Russia directly.'[107] But, there was a hidden agenda and the secret plotting of British Intel could never have survived proper scrutiny by experts.

With restrained irony, a *Russia Today* program commented on 'curious parallels between the plots in *Homeland* and *Strike Back* and the

---

105 On TV, 18.3.22, thesaker.is/maria-zakharova-debunks-british-lies-must-watch/

106 dilyana.bg/uk-defense-ministry-document-reveals-skripals-blood-samples-could-have-been-manipulated/, 3.9.21; johnhelmer.net 'British Defence Ministry document reveals Skripal blood evidence is missing – fake chain of custody makes Novichok evidence worthless,' 5.12.21.

107 RT 7.4.18 'You can't decide in 24 hours.'

media coverage of the Skripal poisoning drama:'[108] In the opening episode a government traitor is assassinated, poisoned with a nerve agent. While it is initially unclear who the culprits are, the episodes that were broadcast on March 4 (the day the Skripals were found) and March 11 make it clear that a Russian intelligence 'active measures' unit were behind the poisoning.

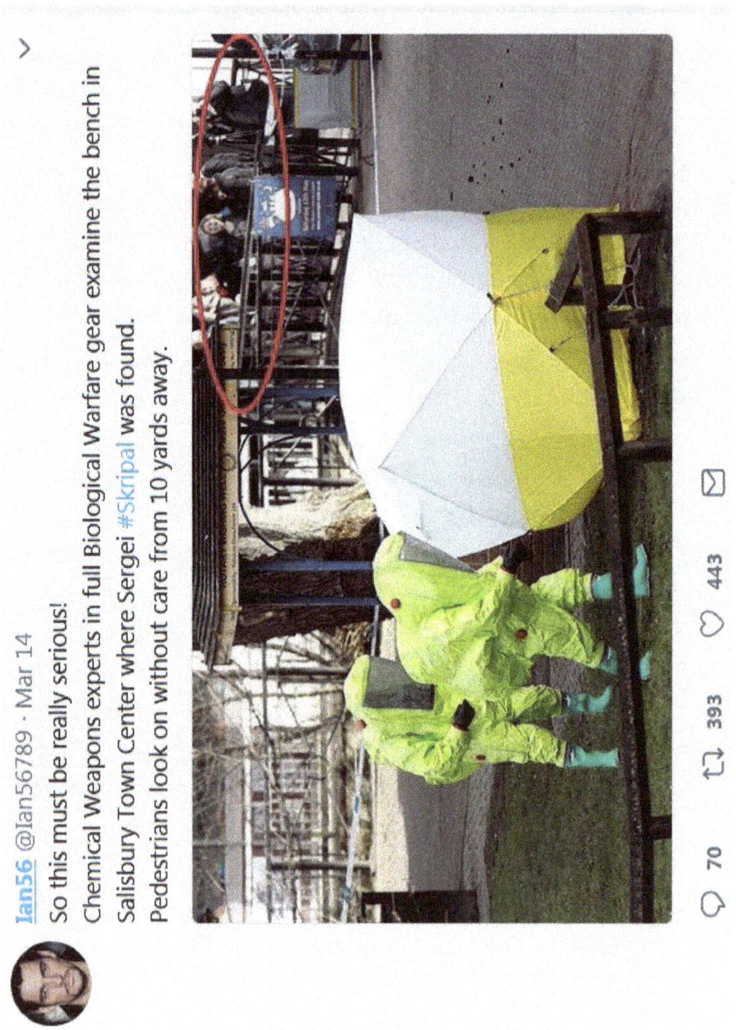

Ian56 @Ian56789 · Mar 14
So this must be really serious!
Chemical Weapons experts in full Biological Warfare gear examine the bench in Salisbury Town Center where Sergei #Skripal was found.
Pedestrians look on without care from 10 yards away.

70 393 443

Figure: Removal of the park bench

108 Sputniknews.com11 April 'How TV Spy Fiction Helped Sell the Salisbury Poisoning'

A later episode had an FBI agent, Dante Allen, turned by Russian intelligence, then unmasked by our hero Carrie Mathison, who then poisons him with a nerve agent to trick him into thinking he is going to die and to make him confess! The next episode broadcast on April 8 showed Dante recovering in hospital, with the Russian assassin demanding that his superiors let him assault the hospital to get to the agent …

Figure: A witty image appeared in *The Times* on April 5th, entitled 'UK locates source of Salisbury nerve agent.' Even a British journalist, it would appear, can experience a desire to tell the truth.

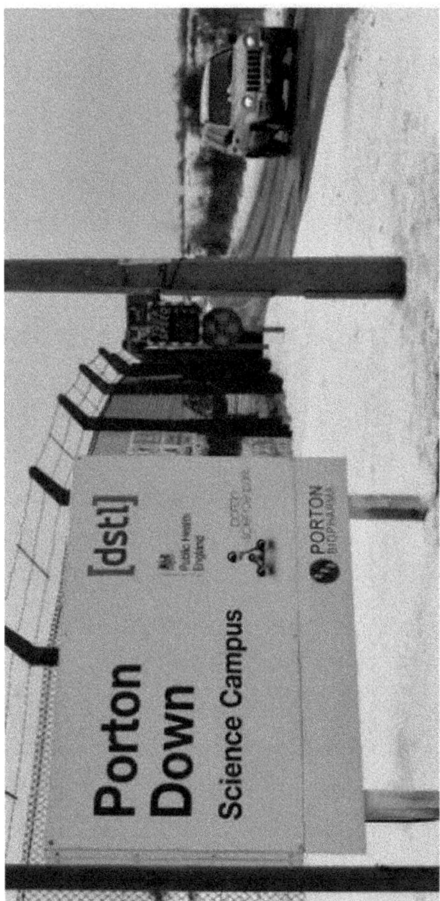

UK locates source of Salisbury nerve agent

Security services believe they have pinpointed the location of the covert Russian laboratory that manufactured the weapons-grade nerve agent used in Salisbury,...

thetimes.co.uk

Apr 05, 2018

On the same day the British media were reporting that the Skripals, who were still in hospital, were so terrified of the Russian assassins that they were going to be given new lives and new identities in America. The irony was not lost on the 'Moon of Alabama' blogger: "Isn't it astonishing how 'life' follows the course of last week's TV drama?"[109]

109 www.moonofalabama.org 'The British Governments 'Novichok drama' was written by whom?'

The OPCW were supposedly given a sample of the fabled Novichok wiped off from the door-handle. They commented that the sample was 'of high purity' which was probably their way of saying that they reckoned it had come straight from Porton Down[110] - which it probably had.

Russia tried to invoke the terms of Chemical Weapons Convention, since both Russia and the UK had signed and ratified it. Clearly it was designed for just such a dispute. Both parties, article 9 explained, should 'first make every effort to clarify and resolve, through exchange of information and consultations amongst themselves, any matter which may cause doubt about compliance…' and when a dispute arises, 'the parties concerned shall consult together with a view to the expeditious settlement of the dispute by negotiations..' (Article 14 section 2). That seemed straightforward enough - Russia made such an appeal at an OPCW meeting on March 13th. The Russian ambassador to London 'had been summoned and asked to provide an explanation' (of what?) Britain's Foreign Secretary averred that 'Russia has provided no explanation, and no meaningful response' (12 March, Helmer p.54). Thus the British government was not interested in the terms of this treaty. Instead, what the US-UK called the 'rules-based international order' was invoked, which more or less means, ask us and we'll tell you what the rules are.

Turning the pages of Mark Urban's book on the Skripal saga, one had hoped to discern how the and the British establishment had reached their conclusion of Russian guilt. But all he says is that

> if it [the UK] had specific intelligence about how the Skripal operation was mounted, the UK was not releasing it...'

Uh-huh. We also gather that the director of Porton Down told Sky News that 'his labs had not been able to trace the Salisbury Novichok samples to Russia,'[111] on April 3rd. I challenge any reader to peruse Mark Urban's book and find an iota of evidence for the accusation, that 'Russia did it:' all we get is hearsay and innuendo without substance.

---

110 Craig Murray, 'Ten Points' (ref 1) 7.3.19.

111 *The Skripal files*, pp. 252, 261.

There exists a consensus, that this crime was an act of state-fabricated terror: that is to say, a state was responsible. Conclusive proof that the crime of abducting two Russian citizens and possibly poisoning them on 4 March 2018 was an act of *British* state-fabricated terror comes from the CCTV footage, or rather its absence. The vanishing of CCTV is a defining feature of modern state-fabricated terror: it *always* happens in such events.[112] To quote John Helmer here,

> Every image of Sergei and Yulia Skripal from the four cameras trained on the bench where they collapsed, and the half-dozen cameras in the pub where Skripal was before the bench, and where he first appeared to witnesses to be unsteady on his feet, remain secret.[113]

All CCTV in Salisbury was working normally on that day however their data have been confiscated by the London counter-terrorism police. No foreign state, it hardly needs saying, can cause such vanishing of all the local CCTV.[114]

Neither of the Skripals have ever made any statement indicating that they accept the 'Russia-did-it' narrative; and Julia has expressed a desire to return to Russia which she would hardly have done if she believed her country had attempted to poison her. These things argue against Russian culpability however they are not conclusive. Only the CCTV evidence can be described in this way, as conclusively indicating Russian innocence.

Letter from an honest man

In the first week after the event, harrowing tales were appearing in the media about how dozens of Salisbury residents were being affected by this nerve agent. The scary headlines ended after a carefully-worded letter appeared in *The Times,* from a senior medic at Salisbury general hospital, on 16th of March:

---

112 NK, *False Flags over Europe, A History of State-fabricated terror,* 2018.
113 Helmer, *Skripal in Prison,* p38.
114 Helmer, Ibid. For further discussion of CCTV see Chapter 14.

> Sir,
>
> Further to your report ("Poison exposure leaves almost 40 needing treatment", March 14), may I clarify that no patients have experienced symptoms of nerve gas poisoning in Salisbury and there have only been three patients with significant poisoning. Several people have attended the emergency department concerned that they may have been exposed. None has had symptoms of poisoning and none has needed treatment. Any blood test performed have shown no abnormality. No member of the public has been contaminated by the agent involved.
>
> Stephen Davies

After that straightforward testimony from a local medic, the stories evaporated, they vanished like a dream – they just had not happened!

Somewhat in response to this letter, Britain's 'Off-Guardian' reached its position of radical scepticism. Referring to Novichok as 'still largely mythical,' it advised:

> Extreme scepticism is required here. An undisclosed agenda is driving things and driving them so hard even members of the political establishment are concerned... almost immediately upon this incident occurring a media campaign of almost unprecedented intensity began to generate what looked like a pre-prepared story that the Skripals had been poisoned by Russia. This claim has been "supported" by untruths and manipulations so questionable even anonymous FCO [Foreign and Commonwealth Office] sources are worried... The government and media are lying, leaping to conclusions and propagandising. Their claims about novichoks are unsubstantiated and seem to fly in the face of all published research. The media are trying to work up a jingoistic anti-Russia hysteria that has no parallel in recent times. Not even the 2003 media frenzy to get public opinion behind the illegal war on Iraq reached these heights. (16 March: 'UK's "Novichok" program exposed as lies')

Discerning British citizens have had two reliable sources to consult over the whole affair: the *Off-Guardian* and the blog of ex-British diplomat Craig Murray. *That's about all,* and these sources have so to speak rescued our sanity amidst the maelstrom of lies from HM Government.

But, the story of local poisonings refused to die and a 'duckpond' tale surfaced a week later: the Skripals standing by their local duckpond had given bread to some youngsters to feed the ducks. The lads had become ill, and *The Sun* told its readers how a 12-year old lad was 'too scared to go out now' after the 'terrifying attack.' (28.3.18). A year later (18 April 2019) the *New York Times* revealed how this narrative had been used as a basis for Trump expelling sixty Russian diplomats. Then, local experts denied the story: "No children or animals were harmed in the Novichok attack in Wiltshire last year, health officials have said."[115] The duck-feeding turns out to be quite pivotal to the narrative, and as we'll see it occurred around 1.45 i.e. right after they parked their car and before they reached the Zizzi restaurant. The point here is that if Sergei really had been contaminated by Novichok, then so also would the youngsters have been contaminated. If the roof of the Skripals' house was removed and the Zizzi restaurant likewise deconstructed, then how come the ducks were unaffected?

The duck story re-surfaced a year later when the President of the United States, no less, was moved by the tale (Chapter 15). How very appropriate that the newspapers should then publish a picture of the wrong duckpond, the one in the prestigious Queen Elizabeth Gardens - nowhere near where the Skripals are supposed to have been on that day: *O what a tangled web we weave…*

Jeremy Corbyn responds

'We don't do fantasy politics' was the initial response from the French government's spokesperson, after Theresa May announced that the Russian diplomats were to be expelled, adding that it would need 'firm proof' of Russian involvement before it gave support. But alas this commendable *sang froid* did not last long, and only a day later on March 15th without any additional evidence coming to light, France joined in

115 The Guardian, 18 April, 'No children or ducks harmed by novichok, say health officials'

with the US, UK and Germany in blaming Russia for the alleged poisoning of the two Skripals.

Likewise, the British opposition leader Jeremy Corbyn cautiously warned against taking steps against Russia without first presenting evidence, and he ventured to call the intelligence on the matter 'problematic.' (March 14th) He urged a 'calm, measured approach' and warned against 'a new cold war.' Russian culpability had not been proved he explained (March 16th) – ah, the words of a real statesman.

At once he found himself being assaulted in a vicious propaganda campaign: a BBC *Panorama* discussion of the Skripal affair took place against a photoshopped background of him wearing a Russian hat in Moscow's Red Square. The tweet from 'Integrity Initiative' as shown below dubbed him a 'useful idiot' working for the Kremlin. All this was merely on account of his hesitation in accepting the Government's narrative, and sensibly requesting that Parliament should first ask to be given some evidence linking Russia to the Novichok story.

One is shocked that anonymous, Government-funded persons can make such defamatory accusations with impuunity. The venom emanating from such sources as 'Integrity Initiative,' against people who were doubting the Government's

Integrity Initiative
@InitIntegrity
Follow
Skripal poisoning: It's time for the Corbyn left to confront its Putin problem
politics.co.uk/comment-analys ... via
@politics_co_uk

narrative, has been effective in preventing rational discussion of the Skripal affair, ensuring that a pre-ordained blame-Russia response prevailed. The hate-and-fear thereby generated enables the mainstream consensus to pass unchallenged: a 'Phantom Menace' *which does not actually exist* is mocked up, whereby the evil behavior attributed to it has actually come from some echelon of British Government or some military arm thereof. In this way dissenting voices can be smeared as somehow collaborating with it.

But too soon, alas, Corbyn folded and endorsed the Government's view, going even beyond it and affirming: "the nerve agent used has been identified as of original Russian manufacture." Even Theresa May had not said that! Her weasel words had only been, that it was 'of a type developed by Russia.'

Jeremy Corbyn's sickening support of Soviet empire
I remember the StB clearly. The Státní Bezpecnost, or State Security, was a pervasive part of my life in Communist-era Czechoslovakia. As the lone...
thetimes.co.uk
Integrity Initiative
@InitIntegrity
Follow
"Mr Corbyn was a "useful idiot", in the phrase apocryphally attributed to Lenin. His open, visceral anti-westernism helped the Kremlin cause, as surely as if he had been secretly peddling Westminster tittle-tattle for money..."
4:19 AM - 23 Feb 2018

Figures: poisonous, hate-filled anti-Corbyn tweets from *Integrity Initiative*

On March 14th, a couple of days after Theresa May's accusation against Russia, Corbyn found himself being denounced in the Commons because of a very sensible comparison he was making, between the Skripal allegation and the UK Government's 'Dodgy dossier' of some years earlier, which had started the Iraq war. He further asked, should not the OPCW have first been consulted? Many in his own Labour party were angrily denouncing him, as if Russian guilt had been established.

Russian Diplomats Expelled

Three weeks after the event, May announced "the largest collective expulsion of Russian intelligence officers in history" and NATO nations were happy to follow suite. One hundred and fifty were expelled, followed by tit-for-tat Russian expulsions so that some *three hundred* diplomats were expelled. How was it possible, after the cooked-up WMD dossier produced by British Intel in 2003 which got the Iraq war going, that international diplomats were *again* prepared to take the word of a British government?

What possible motive could the Russians have for doing such a thing? In June Russia was hosting the World Cup, and a scandal like this was the very last thing it needed. Skripal had been released to live in Salisbury as a result of a spy-swap, and it was the established ethic of such deals that spies thus released had to be left alone afterwards.

A Chinese view is here of interest (*Global Times,* 27 March):

> The British government did not provide evidence that linked Russia to the crime but was confident from the beginning there could be no other "reasonable explanation" for the attempted assassination.... The fact that major Western powers can gang up and "sentence" a foreign country without following the same procedures other countries abide by and according to the basic tenets of international law is chilling. ...
>
> It is beyond outrageous how the US and Europe have treated Russia. Their actions represent a frivolity and recklessness that has grown to characterize Western hegemony that only knows how to contaminate international relations.

Too right! It seemed that Britain no longer had diplomats, and that international diplomacy had been replaced by insults and name-calling by boorish UK officials - who would merely smirk at Russian appeals to due process and international conventions.

On whose word could one rely? Many turned to former British diplomat Craig Murray for guidance and 'Thedeepstate.com' wondered in this context, "Is former British Ambassador Craig Murray the only ujjknowledgeable and honest person the UK government can produce?

It certainly seems that way." Murray's view was that 'If they exist at all, Novichoks were allegedly designed to be able to be made at bench level in any commercial chemical facility' and he quoted the ex-Soviet scientist Mizayanov: "One should be mindful that the chemical components or precursors of A-232 or its binary version novichok-5 are ordinary organophosphates that can be made at commercial chemical companies."[116]

Insofar as they exist, these would be a fairly unremarkable group of organic compounds. Murray has called out Boris Johnson, then Britain's Foreign Secretary, as being an outright liar on this matter.[117] In retrospect, everything stated by Craig Murray on this topic has so far turned out to be correct… and that is a reputation worth having.

A few days before the expulsion of Russian diplomats, a court judgement published a sworn statement by Porton Down from their analysis:

> Porton Down Chemical and Biological Analyst blood samples from Sergei Skripal and Yulia Skripal were analysed and the findings indicated exposure to a nerve agent or related compound. The samples tested positive for the presence of a Novichok class nerve agent or closely related agent.

– from which Craig Murray concluded,

> This sworn Court evidence direct from Porton Down is utterly incompatible with what Boris Johnson has been saying. The truth is that Porton Down have not even positively identified this as a "Novichok", as opposed to "a closely related agent". Even if it were a "Novichok" that would not prove manufacture in Russia, and a "closely related agent" could be manufactured by literally scores of state and non-state actors.
>
> This constitutes irrefutable evidence that the government have been straight out lying – to Parliament, to the EU, to NATO, to the

116 14th March, Craig Murray 'The Novichok Story Is Indeed Another Iraqi WMD Scam.' In the earlier-mentioned TV thriller program, one heard of this 'binary' weapon concept, whereby two harmless substances are mixed together to produce the nerve poison.
117 Craig Murray, 22 March: 'Boris Johnson A Categorical liar.'

United Nations, and above all to the people – about their degree of certainty of the origin of the attack.[118]

Initially, one gathered, Trump was reluctant to expel the Russian diplomats. But then, the CIA's director (on or around the 23rd of March) reportedly showed him some fake photographs of young children in hospital, who had been poisoned by the Salisbury attack, plus some pictures of dead ducks likewise caused by the deadly Novichok. The heart of the US President was moved by these stories and he went along with what the CIA director told him was the 'strong option,' of expelling sixty Russian diplomats.[119] The US President was then furious to discover he had been pressured to expel sixty, when European nations had expelled much smaller numbers.[120]

Two Russian 'Tourists'

In September, the Crown Prosecution Service announced that two Russians Alexander Petrov and Russlan Boshirov were the guilty culprits. How had this discovery taken them six months? The two Russians had visited Salisbury on the 3rd and 4th of March. From the time of their arrival in Salisbury they could have reached the house a little after noon – if that was where they were going. Had they done this, they surely would have had to be sure that Mr Skripal was not at home: they could hardly take the risk of him being in his office which faced up the cul-de-sac road, where he could see any visitors coming.

To place the toxin on the doorknob the two would have needed serious protective clothing, otherwise they would have been poisoned (for photos of the green outfits worn by the police see page 72. The police never provided evidence for anything resembling this. It is clear that no such event ever took place.

---

118 Craig Murray, 'Boris Johnson a categorical liar' 22 March (site now blocked).

119 *The Guardian* 16.4.19 'Novichok poisonings.' Craig Murray, 16.4.19 'The Official Skripal Story is a Dead Duck.'

120 See Chapter 16. For a US discussion of 'Duckgate' (Gina Haspel showing fake photos to the US President) see 'the Duran – News in Review' 20.4.19 www.youtube.com/watch?v=Ll_uPRywcNg

The BBC correspondent Karen Gardner recalled how, a couple of days after the incident, police officers had been mingling around the Skripals' front door -

> When I was here a year ago, I watched Wiltshire police officers with no or minimal protective clothing going in and out that front door. They were carrying coffee flasks. They appeared to have had refreshments in the house overnight. That was two days after the Skripals had collapsed, at the point the Met had taken over the investigation. Shouldn't those officers have been better protected?[121]

This conclusively refutes the official story.

The two Russians had flown over from Moscow on Friday, 2nd March and returned on Sunday the 4th. Six months later, the police alleged that the hotel room the two had stayed in was contaminated with Novichok[122] - the only scrap of evidence ever produced for this accusation. But why had they taken so long to reveal this? The owner of the hotel was taken aback by the news, protesting that he had known nothing about it until 4th September when the story broke. He 'had not been told' of any room in his hotel contaminated with Novichok! Why, wondered Viktoria Skripal, had it taken Britain six months to release details of men charged with attempting to assassinate her uncle Sergei and cousin Yulia in Salisbury?

The two Russians claimed to be weekend tourists, as they explained to RT:

> The two men told Simonyan they went to London to *"hang out,"* and decided to also visit Salisbury upon the advice of their friends. The town, situated close to the world-famous Stonehenge, also attracted them because of the Cathedral Church of the Blessed Virgin Mary, *"famous not just in Europe, but in the whole world."*
>
> Asked about the alleged deadly bottle of perfume, they replied: "Don't you think that it's kind of stupid for two straight men to be carrying perfume for ladies? When you go through customs, they

121 BBC Radio Wiltshire, 6th March.

122 6th September dailymail.co.uk 'Owner of hotel where novichok spies stayed for two nights was only told by police about his killer guests YESTERDAY.'

> check all your belongings. So, if we had anything suspicious, they would definitely have questions. Why would a man have women's perfume in his bag?" Boshirov said.
>
> They also stressed that not only did they not have Novichok in a Nina Ricci bottle, they didn't have it at all, or any other poison for that matter.
>
> Both Petrov and Boshirov sounded distressed as they spoke about how much their lives changed since they were named by the UK as Russian intelligence agents who attempted to assassinate the Skripals. "When your life is turned upside down, you don't really understand what to do and where to go," Boshirov said.[123]

The RT host found the couple to be nervous and perspiring in the studio, so that she had to supply some cognac to 'give them courage.' They did sound rather dopey in the interview, so maybe it was the cognac! They claimed to have some business in the sports and fitness industry but declined to supply details, saying it would compromise their clients. Most people seemed not to believe their story - and it did seem to me that real assassins would have had a better cover story! The intelligence agency 'Bellingcat' tried to claim that these were not their real names and that they worked for Russian intelligence, but I reckon they never showed this.

Scotland Yard was finally able to show CCTV from March 4th, after having been unable to show any for the previous six months: images they released show the two Russians happily pottering around the town in broad daylight. The CCTV shows that they did not catch the train out of Salisbury at 1.41 pm as we were told, but instead are seen wandering about and doing some shopping; they are *not* seen entering the historic old park, where they supposedly discarded the 'perfume bottle', in a bin.

Here is a police photo of the two at 1.05 pm walking down Fisherton road, Salisbury. If this is after they have done the deed, then they seem remarkably cheerful and relaxed, as if they were having a good time. That location is just under a mile away from the home of the Skripals and they are walking in a north-Westerly direction towards the home. At 1.08 pm

123 RT 13.9.18 'We're not agents': UK's suspects in Skripal case talk exclusively with RT's editor-in-chief.

another police photo put them at the junction of Summerlock Approach and Fisherton Street, and we are supposed to gather that they have just come from Christie Miller Road where the Skripals live.

However, the two were captured on a private CCTV video-sequence walking past a shop window, near to the above location on Fisherton street, going past the Dauwalders Coin and Stamp Shop at 1.49 pm., walking towards the train station. This suggests that they were not going anywhere in a hurry, but were just pottering around. This video

belonged to the shop, and its time is incompatible with the police claim that the two reached the Salisbury train station at 1.51pm; they could not have arrived by then.[124]

As was mentioned earlier in Chapter 3, an intelligence source called 'Bellingcat' claimed that the two Russian 'tourists' had three seats booked for the return journey on their plane to Moscow. The suggestion that Mr Skripal had wanted to return to Moscow was confirmed by Vladimir Putin, in an interview with filmmaker Oliver Stone in June 2019:

Stone: What has happened to Skripal? Where is he?

124 'CCTV Footage Shows Petrov & Boshirov Close to the Skripals' The Blogmere 19.9.18: the best website, for local details of the story.

Putin: I have no idea. He is a spy, after all. He is always in hiding.

Stone: They say he was going to come back to Russia. He had some information.

Putin: Yes, I have been told that he wants to make a written request to come back.

Stone: He knew still and he wanted to come back. He had information that he could give to the world press here in Russia.

Putin: I doubt it. He has broken the ranks already. What kind of information can he possess?[125]

This dialogue seems to imply that Skripal is still alive. He did indeed put through three cheerful but non-committal phone calls to his niece Viktoria in Russia on April 4, May 9 and June 26 of 2019; but she found herself unable to return them.

The Synchrony

The two Russians plus Yulia Skripal arrived in Salisbury - having come from Moscow - *within a couple of hours* of each other, in the afternoon of Saturday, 3rd of March. Could this indicate a commonality of intention?

At one O'clock on Sunday march 4th the two Russians were happily strolling over the bridge at the start of Fisherton Road. They were then directly opposite the great old pub, the Mill, at which the Skripals arrived a couple of hours later. Notice how you have never heard anyone point his out before! The Skripals had come from the Zizzi restaurant round the corner, where Sergei had seemed rather stressed and in a hurry to leave after their meal there, as if perchance he had an appointment. That is a close conjunction in space and time, of the four Russians.

At half past one that afternoon the two Skripals had parked their car by 'the Maltings', this being a pleasant, pedestrianised town-centre area where the action takes place in our story. At 1.45 they are seen at a stretch

125 http://en.kremlin.ru/events/president/news/61057 'Interview with Oliver Stone,' 19 July 2019

of the Avon river that flows through the Maltings area by a children's playground, and were feeding the ducks. That place and time was verified by Rob Slane who interviewed the parents of Aidan, a young child who was there. He was given some bread to feed the ducks by Sergei Skripal - a very crucial part of the story, for several reasons: had Sergei picked up Novichok from his front door handle he would then have poisoned both the ducks and the little boy Aidan. Some weeks later Britain's Prime Minister Theresa May assured the President of America Donald Trump that the ducks had been killed! And that therefore he should expel Russian diplomats - which he did! (see next Chapter)

At 1.49 the two Russians are caught on CCTV pottering around outside a stamp shop, still on the Fisherton Road and a mere stone's throw from where they had been earlier. They are *a mere hundred yards* or so from where the two Skripals were, a few minutes earlier, located in the Maltings. Spies meeting by a duckpond is classic John le Carré. They could well have met up, in which case why were the authorities at such pains to avoid having this recognized?

We can at last appreciate why the CCTV images of that day can never be released, namely that the authorities did not want the close conjunction of these Russians in the town centre to be recognised. If the four of them met for example upstairs in the Mill pub, might they have discussed if Sergei wanted to return to Russia and if so what would have to be done? Instead the authorities wished to overlay their false narrative of Russians poisoning an ex-spy: a re-run the of the Litvinenko story that had so successfully wrecked East-West relations twelve years earlier.

Therefore, the authorities published a CCTV image of the two Russians entering Salisbury Station with a fake time added of 1.50 pm. that afternoon. That became part of their story, that the two had applied poison to the Skripal's door at Christie Miller Road at between 12.30 – 1 pm then disposed of their poison bottle and rushed straight back to the railway station. The world believed that until Rob Slane ascertained that CCTV of Fisherton Road was available from a historic old stamp shop. It showed the two Russians on the pavement in front of the shop.[126] Thus, two crucial pieces of research by Rob Slane have enabled us to ascertain

[126] The blogmire.com 'CCTV footage shows Petrov and Bolshirov close the the Skripals,' 19.9.19

What Really Happened and cut through the official misinformation: he interviewed the mother of one of the children who received bread from Sergei, then he obtained and highlighted this private shop CCTV on the main Fisherton Road.

For the police to release a CCTV image from Salisbury station with its timestamp deleted and a fake time written beneath, demonstrates a high demonstrates a high level of deception: it indicates *state complicity.*

Figure: CCTV from Salisbury rail station on March 4th, showing the two Russians with time given of 13.51pm. N.B. they are both facing the wrong way for entering the station!

Confiscation of CCTV or tampering with its images is *the hallmark* of state-fabricated terror. The two Russians entered the security check-in system at Heathrow Airport at 7.28 that evening and so leaving at such an early hour would have been pointless, they would just have had to hang about in an airport lounge. Instead they enjoyed being in Salisbury – which they had come all the way from Russia to visit – that afternoon.

The photo releases to the papers of the child Aidan with parents (see next chapter) was by a duckpond in the main Queen Elizabeth Gardens where one can see the bridge behind them. That is *not* where they actually were, and is some distance away from it: again it is thanks to Rob Slane interviewing the mother that this was clarified. That published image would have greatly thrown off any investigator as regards the close proximity, of the four Russians, at 1.45 in the afternoon.

Dead Ducks and the 'Special Relationship'

The whole cost for Salisbury police had been well above ten million pounds. That may seem a lot to pay for one more pack of lies from the British government - but for the sacred cause of starting a new cold war against Russia, maybe it was all worthwhile.

A year later, in April of 2019, the *New York Times* revealed how the newly-appointed Director of the CIA had persuaded Trump to expel the Russian diplomats: she had shown him pictures of kids in hospital plus some dead ducks at the Salisbury pond. Novichok had done this, she asssured him. She, Gina Haspel, has a reputation for the thrill she obtains from seeing people tortured at Guantanamo. She had been appointed to her new position about ten days after the Skripal story appeared, and then towards the end of the month the stories of children at the duckpond seeing the Skripals on or just after noon, broke. Why, they were given bread from the Skripals contaminated with the deadly Novichok that had come straight from the doorhandle – or so it was stated in the *Mirror, Sun* and *Mail*. Have they no shame? The doyen of US torturers thus moved the heart of her President, to endorse what she called the 'strong option' of expelling sixty diplomats.

The *New York Times* article provoked a response from the director of public health at Wiltshire Council, Tracy Daszkiewicz:

> There were no other casualties other than those previously stated. No wildlife were impacted by the incident and no children were exposed to or became ill as a result of either incident (18 April).

As well as that categoric denial, Salisbury hospital put out a similar statement, that 'no children were admitted as a result of being exposed to Novichok.' The question here arises as to who is lying and who gave the false narrative to the CIA that was used as a basis for the expulsion of Russian diplomats. *The Sun* posted an image of a child at the pond (See below). A local resident realized that this was *the wrong pond*[127]: it

127 www.theblogmire.com, 'It's the wrong park!' 10.7.18

depicts the main green area of Salisbury which is the historic Queen Elizabeth gardens, and that is nowhere near the Maltings, where the Park Bench of Doom was located. In their itinerary, the Skripals had no time to visit that park.

Rob Slane spoke to the mother of one of the boys, Mrs Cooper, who recalled how the police had shown her "really clear" CCTV footage of this incident: she there saw Mr Skripal and his daughter (who she said was carrying a red bag). She said she thought that the time on the CCTV showed 1:15pm, but her partner said it was 1:45m. None of this alleged CCTV has been made public.

Figure: Twelve-year old Aiden Cooper & parents, by duck pond: *The Sun* 28th March (N.B. this is not where he saw the Skripals.)

The newspaper articles on the young boys who were given bread by the Skripals to feed the ducks appeared over 24-28th of March, with the *Sun* quoting the father Luke as to how they did not suspect anything was wrong until the police turned up two weeks later. His son Aiden is quoted as saying that he is scared, too scared to go out, whereas his Father says: "We didn't think anything of it until two weeks later when the police knocked on our door."[128] No problem was perceived until the police arrived two weeks later and started scaring everyone. The CIA Director gave Trump the dead-ducks-and-poisoned-children story around the 20th-23rd which was immediately before it hit the headlines: probably necessary as those newspapers did carry statements that the medical tests were indicating that no poisoning had been detected.

128 *The Sun*, 28 March, 'Schoolboy, 12, on how he was exposed to a deadly poison..'

Two years later, a cache of phone call records between Trump and May were released by *The Telegraph*, (5.9.20) and they featured the British Prime Minister trying to sell the dead duck story to the world's most powerful man – on 13th of March! That is, as Rob Slane pointed out, a week before the new CIA director Gina Haspel was likewise using it, and days *before* any police turned up at young Aidan's door.[129]

Commendably, Trump was resisting pressure from May to believe the British story and act upon it:

> Mrs May was seeking solidarity from the White House over a chemical attack on British soil. But leaked notes from one call between Mr Trump and Mrs May reveal how hard he pushed back. 'We really need your leadership on this', Mrs May said, according to the notes. 'No, I would rather follow than lead,' Mr Trump is quoted responding.
>
> 'Three children fell ill after feeding ducks there', she is quoted saying, referring to the hospitalisation of children who had been in the park where Mr Skripal was found. 'Yes, it's horrible and disgusting', Mr Trump agreed. 'The US and the UK must stand together on this', Mrs May said, according to the notes.

This phone call on the 13th of March was followed by the Russian diplomats expelled on the very next day from the UK, and then on the 26th of March from Europe and America. Only *after* that call were Aidan Cooper and his parents contacted by the police, taken to hospital and found not to have been poisoned. That is to say the least a rather strange sequence of events. No children had fallen ill nor did anybody see any dead ducks.

Private investigator Rob Slane contacted the mother of Aidan who was very helpful, confirming to him that her family had seen the two Skripals feeding ducks at the duckpond at around 1.45 pm on that day and that the girl had been carrying a red bag, as other reports also confirmed. She also said that when the police later came round to interview Aidan, they showed CCTV footage of the Skripals at the duckpond, feeding ducks and handing bread to three local boys, one of whom ate it. That CCTV cannot be released for an obvious reason: were the Novichok story true, then there *would have been* both dead ducks and

---

129 www.theblogmire.com 'trump in dumps' 16.4.19.

sick or dying children. In fact, *none* of the people who came into direct contact with the Skripas tested positive for Novichok.

This extraordinary sequence of events features the US President pressured into expelling a huge number of diplomats by his CIA Director, after he had earlier resisted such pressure from Theresa May. Only after the President had been given that story did British police visit the Cooper family. So who created the bogus dead-duck story and the fake pictures used by the CIA director? Is this how transatlantic intelligence is shared?

The Skripal story has been used to degrade diplomacy and ramp up a new cold war against Russia. MI6 plans for the isolation and economic ruin of Russia, including sporting bans and ending cultural exchanges, date from 2015, as revealed by a collective called 'Anonymous'. In 2019 it emerged that Mark Urban had been receiving secret service sponsorship to interview Skripal months *before* the March 4th incident. He just happened to be writing a biography of the Russian double-agent, when to his surprise …

British newspapers are by far the least trusted amongst EU readers. This emerged from a survey of 33 European nations in 2017, with a thousand people surveyed in each country, showing that rock-bottom level of trust in British media[130].

Foreign Secretary Boris Johnson affirmed that:

> British intelligence has a copy of the Russian training manual, which includes instruction on painting nerve agent on doorknobs.[131]

He had seen a copy, he stated; which was however much too secret to show anyone. Did any paper criticize such casual mendacity? On the contrary, he was admired for his ability to grab headlines, and has since become the Prime Minister.

What a shame we could not be shown this Russian manual for poisoning door knobs. Does it say that it is best done with an atomised aerosol?

---

130 Press Gazette UK 26.5.17 'Survey finds that UK written press is least trusted in Europe'
131 Murray, 'Holes in the Official Skripal Story', 12 July.

As of July 2019, *Russia Today* was fined £200,000 by Ofcom for 'lack of balance' in its programmes. Primarily, this was a result of some well-balanced comments upon the Skripal affair made by the irrepressible George Galloway on his weekly program 'Sputnik.' The British government's narrative had been "sadly in want of consistency and accuracy" he stated – and who could disagree? His guest on the program was former Kremlin advisor Alexander Nekrassov, who reckoned that the incident was a "badly prepared provocation": British politicians were "in trouble" in his view and needed a distraction. He was here merely giving expression to a widespread view, that the whole affair had been designed to distract the public from the frustrating Brexit process.

A month later in August 2019 the US imposed a fresh round of sanctions against Russia, on the basis of the Skripal story, whereby US banks would be prohibited from issuing loans to Russia, and the US would try to stop international banks from doing so.

We are all left wondering, is Yulia still alive? In September of 2020 we heard that she was keeping healthy 'walking in the fields' from a phone call to her cousin Viktoria. She did not indicate her location. Since then there have been no further phone calls: only a deep silence, as neither she nor her father responded to news of the death of her Mother a few months later.

A Lovely New Yulia

Let's come back to that last afternoon, when the Skripals enjoyed a drink together. One can discern the photographer reflected in the mirror behind them. Media sources later obscured this 'man in the mirror' image, after the D-notices banning any allusion to Pablo Miller had appeared; which would tend to suggest that the image was taken on that day by Pablo Miller. A couple of other images of father and daughter have been released, enjoying a drink together. We note Yulia's face, which is plump and round, with hair parted on the left.

Figures: the old, pre-Novichok Yulia

A month later, on April 5th a phone call from Yulia to her cousin Viktoria in Russia came out with the news that the couple were OK and recovering and that she hoped to return to Russia! While still in hospital, did she borrow somebody's mobile phone and call her cousin in Moscow?[132] 'I woke up over a week ago' she said - implying that they had been in a coma for several weeks: *Later, let's talk later. In short, everything is OK. He's resting now, he's sleeping* [i.e. her father]. *Everyone's health is OK. No one has had any irreversible [harm]. I'm being discharged soon.*

132 For text see: Mark.Urban, *The Skripal files*, pp.266-7.

Viktoria can be heard telling her cousin *"If I get my visa tomorrow, on Monday I will fly to you"* and Yulia responds, *"nobody will give you a visa."* One sensed that this call was rather believable. Sure enough, the British government did refuse to grant a visa to Viktoria: why would it not want Yulia's very close relative to come and console her, at this most stressful moment in her life??

After all the government stories of how deadly the stuff was, plus the accusation of murder made against Russia with all of NATO expelling its diplomats, suddenly everything's fine! It was then reported on 8th April, as if in response to this unplanned phone call, that the couple were going to be shipped over to the US with changed identities.

Six weeks after her release from the Salisbury hospital on April 11th, Yulia made her one and only media appearance on 23rd May. A new, slimline Yulia appeared and the world marvelled at the change. She no longer needed glasses and had lost much weight in hospital. Her hair was much thicker and now *parted on the right*. It rustled as she moved her head – had she been having some beauty treatment? The story went viral.

This charming Yulia appears here as improved and younger-looking after the 'Novichok attack'. Gone is the old, frumpy Yulia as the rejuvenating Novichok elixir wiped years off her appearance! Verily, British intelligence is a Hall of Mirrors. There was a prominent scar on her thorax, and questioned about that she only remarked that her treatment had been "invasive, painful and depressing."[133]

In her carefully scripted appearance, we see her wandering out of a wood along a winding path, no doubt expressing the magical 'renewal' process. She then sat down and read out a statement, concerning which a Russian embassy spokesman commented: "The video shown only strengthens our concerns as to the conditions in which she is being held. Obviously, Yulia was reading a pre-written text. More than that, judging from quite a few elements, the text was a translation from English and had initially been written by an English-speaker."[134]

Others pointed out that her text *did not blame Russia* – had she

133 The Salisbury doctors told the BBC that 'the Skripals were heavily sedated, to receive artificial ventilation and to protect them from brain damage': bbc.co.uk 29th May, 'How the Skripals were saved.'

134 Mirror, 23 May 'Yulia Skripal appears for first time since Novichok'

Figures: the new, improved Yulia

maybe insisted on that point? On March 21st a Russian source complained, 'Moscow is surprised that UK authorities deny consular access to Skripal's daughter in violation of international norms.'[135]

135 The Salisbury National Health Service Foundation Trust sought leave in a three-day secret

None of her neighbours, friends or relatives had been allowed to see her, not in hospital or anywhere else since March 4th. Not even Ross Cassidy was allowed to see them, and a Russian TV crew which tried to get into Salisbury hospital was thwarted.

Yulia's 89-year old grandmother Yelena, i.e. the mother of Sergei, was being cared for by Viktoria. She received a startling phone call on her 90th birthday:

> She [Julia} called and was actually with Sergei. She told me: "I'm with daddy he is beside me but he can't speak as he has a pain in his throat"... He can't speak because he's got a tracheostomy, that pipe, which will be taken off in three days. Now when he speaks with that pipe, his voice is first of all very weak and secondly, he makes quite a lot of wheeze. He had been in some pain (24th July).

Figure: this joke 'new, improved Yulia' image went viral. Note its 'perfume bottle,' months before the UK police claimed to have found it!

In this conversation, Yulia strangely kept saying to her grandmother, 'Everything is fine, everything is perfect' in a way that some found suspicious. She made no effort to convey a message from Sergei to his mother, which led some to suspect that he was not there.[136]

If what she said was true, that her father was still having the tracheostomy operation, they would have to have been in the hospital. That would be strange, four months after the event, and two months after we were told he had been released from hospital. Nor does the message well accord with her earlier phone call to Viktoria when she had said that her father was fine.

Months later in October, Viktoria confirmed that there had been direct contacts with her cousin Yulia, who planned to return to Russia once her father was better.

Eleven months later, we learnt that the Novichok is still so deadly, that the whole roof of the Skripal's home needs replacing, by yellow-clad

hearing of the Court of Protection (20-22 March) to take blood samples from the 'Skripals' – from which we gather, that even while they were staying in a public hospital, the NHS was unable to obtain blood samples ('the Williams Judgement').

136 *Russia Insider* article by Rob Slane, 'Where is Sergei Skripal?'

security agents wearing military bio-hazard suits etc. First the doorknob, then the roof timbers?

I have given a couple of talks on the subject covered in this booklet showing all of the Yulia pictures to the audiences. I asked their opinion and by a show of hands, a huge majority reckoned that they were two different women, pre- and post- Novichok.

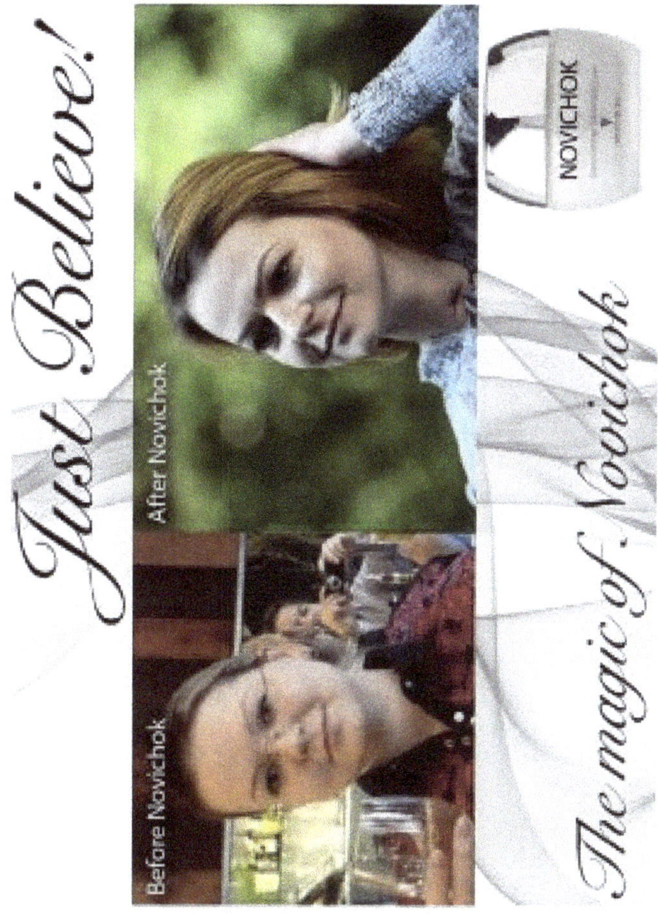

The 'Novichok' bottle of perfume in the illustration is quite precognitive: such an actual bottle - as actual as it ever becomes - will not manifest itself for another few months. It did so in the neighbouring town of Amesbury and soon became an indispensable part of the story (Chapter 13).

Yulia twice stated that *she* had been attacked. On being released from hospital (11th of April) she put out a statement which said, explained, "I find myself in a totally different life than the ordinary one I left just over a month ago, and I am seeking to come to terms with my prospects, whilst also recovering from *this attack on me.*" A month later in the video appearance we've just looked at she repeated this: "After 20 days in a coma, I woke to the news that we had both been poisoned….I still find it difficult to come to terms with *the fact that both of us were attacked. We are so lucky to have both survived this attempted assassination.*"" (23rd May) Never did she say or imply that it was just her father who was attacked and she was just somehow caught up in it. She finds it hard for her to come to terms, not with the fact that she was poisoned, but that she was *attacked*. That rather implies there was a sudden assault with a nerve agent just prior to their park bench collapse. Poisoning with a nerve agent works quickly and it does not take several hours: and, after a prolonged coma as she experienced, one often does not remember the immediate events prior to falling unconscious.

What Yulia has said will prevent her ever being released: she cannot be at liberty to explain what she had meant by her statements.

Death of a Drug-addict

The Skripal's cat had to be put down and by mid-April it appeared as being the only really dead thing in the whole story: or we should say, officially dead, as some were surmising it had merely been taken to Yulia, wherever she was.

The story was threatening to become humorous, with discussions about the house cat-flap. Two hundred diplomats expelled by NATO nations around the world, massive sanctions against Russia being prepared, and only a cat has died? In mid-March at the United Nations the UK justified the expulsion of two dozen Russian diplomats by describing the nerve agent as "a weapon so horrific it is banned from use in war." Then Yulia declared they were both fine … It became evident that, in order to restore *gravitas* to the British story, a real death was needed. How could that be arranged, four months after the event? An answer was found, in the form of a homeless drug-addict staying in a hostel in Salisbury called Dawn Sturgess.

Figure: Only the cat had died?

A friend described Ms Sturgess as being a homeless alcoholic who suffered from post-natal depression after her son Aidan was born, who had been smoking weed and over the course of time had turned to harder drugs - she had become 'like a zombie.'[137] Her partner Charlie Rowley was housed at a hostel in Muggleton Road, Amesbury. One night she "was on the floor having a fit and foaming at the mouth" and soon Charlie Rowley was experiencing similar symptoms. The police assumed that they were ill due to a contaminated batch of drugs, or maybe overdosing on heroin or crack cocaine.

Unconscious, she was taken by ambulance to Salisbury hospital at 10.30 in the morning of Sunday, July 1st. The next day Wiltshire police issued warnings by twitter and their official website confirming that their search of the Sturgess-Rowley flat in Amesbury, together with interviews of others who were in the flat at a party the evening before Dawn's collapse,

137 Holly Christodoulou *The Sun* 22.11.18 'Poison Death: Who was Dawn Sturgess'?

confirmed that Sturgess and Rowley had "fallen ill after using a contaminated batch of drugs possibly heroin or crack cocaine." They therefore advised other drug users to be 'extra cautious.'

Police tweet for 2nd July:

We are issuing an urgent warning to drug users in the south of Wiltshire after two people fell seriously ill in #Amesbury over the weekend. Read more: goo.gl/TU4Zfz

The *Salisbury Journal* on 2nd July had the headline, 'Police warn drug users after contamination leaves two in hospital.' Then police on the 3rd of July issued a warning, here shown. There was no doubt in this police report about the 'major incident' in which a couple treated by the emergency services were found to have taken 'contaminated drugs.'

One day later, the whole story changed: in London the Metropolitan police's Chief Assistant Commissioner Neil Basu announced on the BBC News that the two of them had been poisoned by 'the same nerve agent' as Sergei Skripal![138] The carefully-researched public statements by the local Wiltshire police about drugs and drug addicts were deleted (the police Warning, above, was recovered by John Helmer using archive.org), but that whole story had suddenly become 'inoperative.' Somehow, the Met in London suddenly know better than the local police about what had happened.

The new Government narrative emerging on July 4th was a shock for the mother of Dawn Sturgess, who had been by her daughter's bedside for the last three nights. She had been informed that the cause of death was heart failure causing oxygen starvation of the brain and felt betrayed with the authorities not telling her the truth.

The new story was unfolded. Mr Rowley was in the habit of going 'bin diving' where he would 'pick up fag butts, go into charity shop bins,' etc. and one day while rummaging in bins of the historic Queen Elizabeth Gardens in Salisbury he picked up a perfume bottle that had somehow

138 www.bbc.co.uk/news 'Amesbury Novichok Poisoning'

been there for several months. It was 'boxed and sealed' in a cellophane wrapper, or so he told *the Guardian*. Because it was 'sealed, boxed and looked expensive' (25th July) he picked it up: "It was an oily substance and I smelled it and it didn't smell of perfume." (24th July) Despite this he gave it to his partner as a present – a fatal mistake.

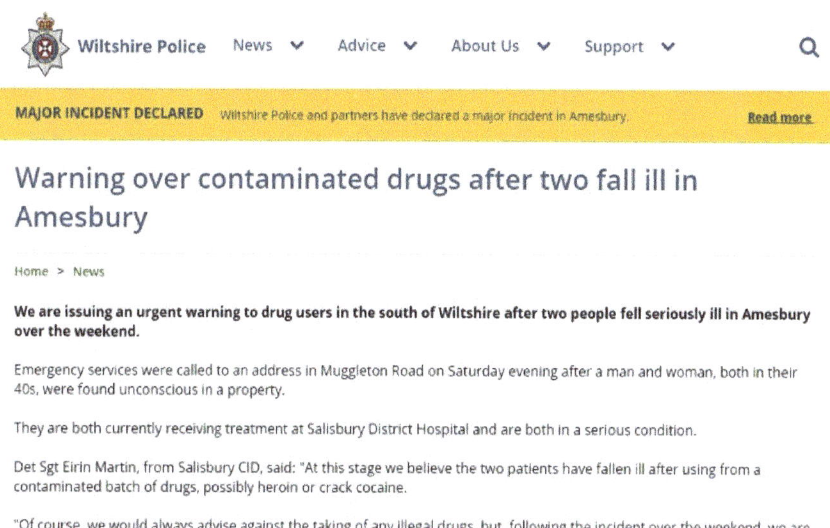
Wiltshire Police News Advice About Us Support

MAJOR INCIDENT DECLARED Wiltshire Police and partners have declared a major incident in Amesbury. Read more

Warning over contaminated drugs after two fall ill in Amesbury

Home > News

We are issuing an urgent warning to drug users in the south of Wiltshire after two people fell seriously ill in Amesbury over the weekend.

Emergency services were called to an address in Muggleton Road on Saturday evening after a man and woman, both in their 40s, were found unconscious in a property.

They are both currently receiving treatment at Salisbury District Hospital and are both in a serious condition.

Det Sgt Eirin Martin, from Salisbury CID, said: "At this stage we believe the two patients have fallen ill after using from a contaminated batch of drugs, possibly heroin or crack cocaine.

"Of course, we would always advise against the taking of any illegal drugs, but, following the incident over the weekend, we are urging drug users to be extra cautious.

"Our main priority is the safety of the public, which is why we have taken this unusual step of issuing this warning about drugs which may be in circulation in the south of the county.

This daft story left a cluster of unanswered questions a-hovering in the public mind: how did a sticky gel turn into a vapour that could be squirted from a bottle? How come park wardens didn't empty the bin for three months? Why would two Russian agents want to stroll through a park that was not on their way to or from wherever they were going, e.g. the train station, and casually toss the deadly poison away? How come whatever they had used magically ended up sealed and unopened like a present? Clearly the perfume bottle did not have their fingerprints on it, or the police would have pressed charges – which they haven't. Was there ever a coroner's report, declaring that death was by Novichok and not just heart failure? That certainly did not appear. Then last but not least, who has got the bottle, if perchance it exists?

It was in the wake of this 'real death' that the US announced their Russian sanctions based upon the Novichok scam, in August (in fact on 8.8.18). A Russian embassy spokesman then stated, 'We have grown accustomed to not hearing any facts or evidence.' The rouble sank to its lowest level for nearly two years. Sagely commented one blogger, *"It looks like the "Novichok" British MI6 Hysteria is being uncorked again, in order to bring more US sanctions against Russia."* ('Hamlet Quest' on *Russian Insider* 8.8.18)

Under British law, where there is a suspicious death, a Coroner's Court hearing must be held, and this clearly applied to the death of Dawn Sturgess. The first such hearing held on 19 July 2018 was immediately adjourned, and then another inquest into her death in January 2019 was also postponed. There was a problem in obtaining the required verdict, despite having received advice from police, military, intelligence and toxicology experts. It seemed that no conclusion could be reached over her death – nor was anyone prepared to comment upon what the alleged perfume bottle contained. Finally in October 2019 the Coroner's Court issued a statement announcing that the inquest into her death had been adjourned indefinitely.

Did this mean that the entire British Novichok story had collapsed, because no-one had died from it? That could not be allowed to happen, and so the coroner's Enquiry on Dawn Sturgess was finally transferred to the High Court of London in 2021. Could Lady Justice Hallett – 'a safe pair of hands' – ensure a proper verdict? Not really it turned out, the Baroness resigned from the job fairly soon after being given it – we return to this saga in the last chapter.

A Strange Bottle of Perfume

> 'We cannot account for the whereabouts of the bottle, nozzle or box between the attack on the Skripals on 4 March 2018 and when Charlie Rowley said he found it on 27 June 2018. Anyone who saw this pink box or glass bottle during this time is asked to call the police…' Neil Basu, Head of UK counter-terror policing, 1.3.19

The above quote shows an honest expression of bewilderment by Neil Basu, the Head of UK's Counter-Terrorism policing. No-one ever saw this 'pink box or glass bottle' prior to June - July of 2018 we here argue, because it did not then exist. The narrative of a Novichok-containing bottle of perfume began to appear around the 3rd week of July and soon became projected back in time: it endures as a central part of the original Skripal story! The following timeline may help.

Dawn Sturgess (DS) & Charlie Rowley (CR), June-July

June 29 CR and DS visit Salisbury to walk in park, do *not* find bottle.

June 30 DS falls into a coma at CR's home, taken to hospital, CR goes on to a hog roast.[139]

July 5 – While both are 'critically ill' in hospital, their poison 'identified' as Novichok

July 8 The *Mirror* avers that CR had found 'a stash of vials or syringes' in the park.

July 8 – DS 'dies' in hospital

July 11 CR wakes up from coma

July 13 Police report having found 'a bottle' on 11th July, in CR's home.

July 17 CR's brother says Charlie 'picked up a perfume bottle in the park.'

July 17 DS post-mortem

July 19 Inquest held for DS death, adjourned.

July 24 – CR starts telling the perfume bottle story on ITV interview

We may here sense the pressure that CR was under, as he awoke from his coma to be told the dreadful news, with his memory quite blurred. The police started to tell him about the bottle, which they had allegedly found in his kitchen and he was not able to deny this or to escape from its implications. He had no choice but to accept their narrative. It is therefore not surprising that -

> Rowley's press interviews have been vague, inconsistent, self-contradictory, and evasive on where the perfume bottle was found, by whom; and when. He and the police have been unable to explain how the perfume bottle on his kitchen table and the package in his kitchen waste bin did not turn up until July 11; that

139 CBC Radio 'Latest Novichok Victim seemed 'drunk' before being hospitalised.' 5.7.18.

was twelve days after Rowley and Sturgess were taken to hospital; and three days after Sturgess's death certificate was signed.[140]

The police could not announce finding the bottle until a couple of days after CR had woken up, because they first had to make sure that he was accepting the *memory-implant* so to speak which they were giving him.

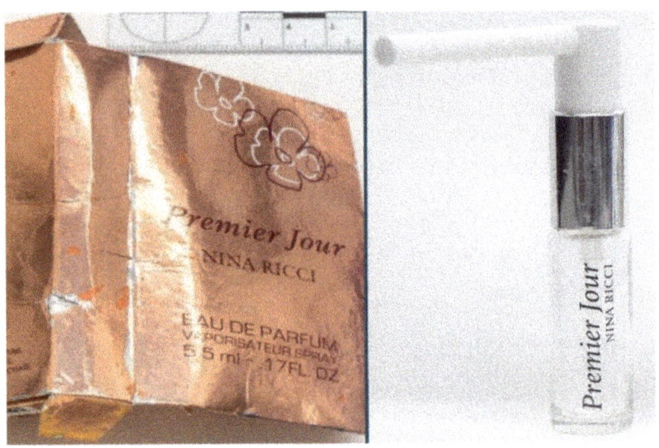

Figure: police photo of bottle plus wrapping

Some reckon that there was a genuine perfume bottle of *Nina Ricci*, shoplifted by Charlie Rowley from Boots while obtaining his methadone prescription (a heroin substitute for recovering drug-addicts). The Salisbury branch did stock the *Nina Ricci* perfumes. That Boots shop was cordoned off and closed by the police for an extended period in the wake of Dawn's death. Maybe he decided to give this present to his partner Dawn Sturgess, but sadly she died from drug-related reasons and her body was conveniently cremated asap.

The unconscious DS was taken off in an ambulance on that Saturday morning (June 30th) to the Salisbury hospital. Her body was held in hospital for a week on life-support, during which period it showed no signs of life.

CR does not accompany her to the hospital, but instead attends an annual barbeque and hog roast on the village green organized by his local Baptist Church that afternoon, albeit he was somewhat the worse for drink and unsteady on his feet: 'Roy Collins, Church secretary of the

140 John Helmer, Dances with Bears, *Skripal Showdown, Novichok Payday* 21.5.20

Amesbury Baptist Centre described how CR stood out from the other people there, in that he seemed inebriated and in a dishevelled condition.'[141] Upon returning home, to quote Mr Neil Basu, 'at 6.20pm, Charlie was also taken ill. The ambulance service was called back to his address and he too was taken to hospital.'[142] Once again, two alleged 'Novichok victims' are lying in a coma at the same hospital as had the Skripals four months earlier.

Charlie Rowley recovered but with sight and balance compromised and he had difficulty sleeping at night. He *denied* having found the bottle in a park: when asked in a TV interview[143] "You're pretty sure when you were in the park on Friday afternoon that you didn't find [the bottle] there?" he replied, "I'm pretty sure. No I'm 100% sure, it wasn't in the park." That 'Friday' alluded to was June 29th, when the couple were visiting Salisbury – that being the day before his partner fell into a coma at his home. In a subsequent ITV interview, where he was filmed being taken around Salisbury, he again expressed confidence that he had not found it in the park.

Though unsure where the bottle had come from, he remained certain that he had *not* found it in the park. While he lay unconscious for over a week in the main Salisbury hospital, the press speculated as to where the poison had come from. During that time Dawn passed away (on 8th July), ie she never regained consciousness. On the same day that he woke up, police reported having found 'the bottle' *in his house*, in Amesbury.

That was on the 11th of July. Earlier, on the 5th we had been informed that the couple were critically ill in hospital, and that the poison had been 'identified' as the same Novichok that had poisoned Skripals. There had been, the *Evening Standard* assured us on that evening, a 'multi-million pound clean up' after the Skripal event, with a hundred counter-terror agents working with Wiltshire police to try and detect, whatever it was that had poisoned them. On the 6th the *Mirror* announced that Charlie had found 'the container' in some bushes in the park, then a couple of days later it said that he had found 'a stash of vials or syringes' while 'scavenging' through bushes. But, those didn't last long: on the 13th we

141 CBCRadio 'Latest Novichok Victim seemed drunk before being hospitalised,'5.7.18
142 Met police Press Release, 1 March 2019.
143 ITV interview of 24th July, The Blogmire

were told that 'a bottle had been found' at Charlie's home, which had tested positive for Novichok and that this had been found on the 11th. That was the first definite police statement about the container. If the police had been conducting an immense, multi-million pound search, how come it took them eleven days to spot a 'bottle' in Charlie Rowley's home, presumably left where the ill-fated couple had passed out?

Charlie's brother endorsed the bush-in-the-park story, and it was he who introduced the perfume bottle motif: the couple had 'picked up a perfume bottle in a park containing the nerve agent and sprayed it on themselves.' (The *Mail*, July 17th) This soon became the accepted narrative even though Charlie himself did not endorse it. On the 19th he claimed that Dawn had sprayed the Novichok on her wrists 'from a discarded perfume bottle she came across on a day out,' then later on he would recall that it was found in a charity shop bin.

On the 24th of July, he gave his shocking account of how well wrapped up in a package the perfume bottle was, so that it had to be an *unused bottle.* The official story died on that day! One can hardly maintain that covert Russian agents first poisoned the two Skripals synchronously then left another, separate bottle of the same deadly poison in a litter bin somewhere else: where that litter bin has to remain miraculously unemptied for four months, while dozens of police and detectives were supposedly scouring the area, to find any clues.

Two Fake bottles?

Another theory has the police *creating* the bottle so it merely resembled a *Nino Ricci* perfume. Mr Basu stated that it had *not* been a *Nino Ricci* bottle but just a lookalike. Why would two Russians want to construct a lookalike bottle of French perfume, put deadly Novichok in it then wrap it up in plastic to look 'unopened'? Or worse, 'Two fake perfume bottles in fact, since the government, police and Coroner Ridley all claim that one bottle was used to attack the door-handle of the Skripal home, and the other was found months later by Rowley, its packaging intact and unopened.'[144]

This is about as mad as anything one could try to imagine. To quote Rob Slane on this matter:

---

144 John Helmer, *Skripal in Prison* 2019 p.292.

> This hypothetical possibility doesn't really need to be refuted; it refutes itself. It's insane. It's completely bonkers. It's risible. It's a joke.[145]

For a feasible decryption of this story, we turn to the blogger 'Milda':

> I would say that in mid-July the handlers of the case had not yet possessed the bottle they needed. At first, they were waiting for Charlie to wake up after sedation, in order to make sure that his memories were vague enough to not contradict their narrative. Meanwhile, or after Charlie's returning to consciousness, the handlers took the trouble of obtaining a perfume bottle that could come exclusively from Russia (like the "Novichok" itself). The result of their search for such a bottle was the counterfeit Nina Ricci perfume bottle of 5.5 ml. The bottle was emptied and then the Porton Down chemists filled it with the same substance which they had used for the Salisbury samples – that substance, according to the OPCW, contained no impurities. But inside the counterfeit Nina Ricci bottle there was a little bit of perfume residue, that's why the Amesbury sample contained 2-3% of impurities.'[146]

The OPCW report dated 4 September described two visits made to Amesbury. On the first (July 15-18) they attended the post-mortem of Ms Sturgess on the 18th and took samples; quite how samples could be taken from a corpse that has been dead for ten days was not explained. Had she ingested Novichok on 30th of June, would it still be detectable 18 days later? The OPCW team returned on 13th of August when they were able to take a 'sample of the contents of a small bottle' which the police declared they had 'seized' from Charlie Rowley's home. This implies that the bottle was not available on their first visit. This answers Milda's question, 'Why did the OPCW team not take their sample from the Nina Ricci bottle while they were in the UK on 15-18 July? When the OPCW did take the sample on 13 August, it turned out to have 2-3% of impurities. Why did the Amesbury sample contain impurities while the Salisbury sample did not?'

On the 5th of September the unlikely-looking design of the 'perfume bottle' was disclosed, shown above, with a nozzle attached. The narrative

145 theblogmire.com/in-memory-of-dawn-sturgess/

146 theblogmire.com/in-memory-of-dawn-sturgess/#comment-30282

had Dawn being 'sprayed' by the well-meaning Charlie who believed it was perfume. Can one believe the bottle here shown would spray' anything? Searching for images of 'Nine Ricci perfumes' one finds nothing resembling this or indeed anything with a nozzle. Again we concur with the perceptive blogger Milda that "As I see it, the only use of the nozzle is to provide an explanation as to how Charlie got contaminated with the "Novichok."

5th September was the day when British newspapers indentified the two Russians as the villains. Those two had carried this invented bottle of perfume, designed such that whoever tries to screw on the nozzle would get poisoned with 'Novichok,' carefully wrapped it up in plastic and dumped it in a rubbish bin somewhere in Salisbury. If you believe that I've got a nice bridge to sell you.

A year after the event Rowley was expressing his stress and anger about how the British authorities 'have not been transparent' about what happened to Dawn Sturgess which is a bit of an understatement. He added, 'I feel like we're being kept in the dark about what really happened,' which is true enough. He reaffirmed that the bottle he picked up was 'sealed with hard plastic' and needed a kitchen knife to open it, which was surely correct: it was good as new. He concluded, quite logically, that 'It can't possibly be the same bottle that was used by the Skripals.'[147]

Rowley was given the hope that he can sue the Russian government for a million pounds. John Helmer made the perhaps unkind comment that: "One consistency in Rowley's record to-date is his hope to make as much money out of telling his story as he can."

We have been given a gradually-unfolding and changing story, which makes very little sense, with a real death *but* no inquest verdict, and one damaged human being remaining who has had a 'memory' imposed upon him. Some years later a revamp of this inquest takes place, in London's High Court of Justice.

---

147 *The Guardian*, 21.6.19 'Novichok victim 'We're being kept in the dark.'

White Helmets at Damascus

The Skripal story required a high level of cognitive dissonance in believers, for which reason it (a) had to continually keep developing, with new additions, as distractions, and (b) was punctuated – to borrow an expression – by the bombing of Syria, where equally spurious claims about chemical weapons were being made. In March and April of 2018, *two different packs of British lies* were blossoming in synchrony, causing far-reaching damage: in Douma, Syria and in Salisbury, England.

The expulsion of Russian diplomats, caused by the Skripal affair, took place just prior to a massive attack upon Damascus on 14th April by US, UK and French airplanes. That attack was in turn prior to the scheduled arrival of the OPCW team in Douma, that being the site of the alleged chemical weapons attack. The OPCW was thereby sidelined, because their visit became fairly meaningless once the whole site had been bombed. It became evident that the UK-founded 'White Helmets' group had set up the phoney CW attack that enabled the bombing: this well-funded group was set up by the British army for such a purpose, whereby it would pretend to be rescuing children from attacks by the Syrian government.

How remarkable that both Syria and Russia have been demonized by these psy-ops: both of them British-fabricated mock-events, which ran concurrently. Both stories concerned chemical weapons, and were presumably related to or deriving from the three-week 'Operation Toxic Dagger' rehearsed by the British Army beforehand on Salisbury Plain. Here is a doctor in the Douma hospital commenting on the White-Helmets masquerade:

> Many people burst into the hospital. Among them were those clad in medical outfit but they were not our employees, and I do not think that they were medics at all. They started shouting something about a chemical attack dousing people with water and all this was filmed. As a result, rumours were spread among Douma residents, something which in turn sparked panic ... (Dr Jaber, Sputnik news.com, 7th April)

This statement, by a doctor in Syria denying that any CW victims had been treated in his hospital, is analogous to the letter sent by a Salisbury doctor to *The Times* a few weeks earlier, denying that any CW victims had been treated in his hospital. Both cases were responding to a deceptive story woven by British military intelligence. One may see a further analogy, in that the OPCW had to be marginalised, in order to prevent it from exposing the phoney White Helmets story, so that the Syrian government could be blamed for the fake CW attack.

President Assad in an interview with *The Mail* stated a couple of months after the event, that 'we consider White Helmets to be a PR stunt by the UK.' Likewise, a BBC Syria producer Riam Dalati tweeted that the whole Douma CW story had been fabricated: 'After almost six months investigations, I can prove without a doubt that the Douma hospital scene was staged.'

KIDNAPPED, NOT SAVED, WHITE
HELMETS TERRORIST AT WORK

Figure: *Veterans Today* image 23.12.18

In response the BBC attempted some damage-control. We quote the insightful Vanessa Beeley from her visit to Syria – interviewed by *Veterans Today* (14.2.19):

> So, fundamentally what these mainstream outlets do is put out a narrative which, as I've pointed out, effectively manufactured consent for the unlawful bombing of a sovereign nation, Syria, by the US, France and the UK, post- the Douma alleged attack. But these storylines and these narratives are never retracted; so it remains to be seen whether the BBC will apologise to Syria for having manufactured the consent for the bombing, and whether Riam Dalati and the BBC will apologise to academics and to independent journalists that they smeared at the time for arriving at the same conclusion they've now arrived at.

I've proven and I've written an open investigation based on testimony from civilians in Eastern Ghouta of the White Helmets staging at least one chemical weapon attack one month before Douma... which was actually derailed by the civilians themselves who exposed it on social media etc. The White Helmets have been proven time and time again to be staging events in order to serve the NATO member states' regime change narrative inside Syria. This might start to raise questions over the veracity of the White Helmets reports, bearing in mind that the UK government document has publicly stated that Amnesty International and Human Rights Watch, for example, rely extensively on the evidence of the White Helmets to produce their reports that, again, largely criminalise the Syrian government.

The very fact that France, the UK and the US went ahead and bombed Syria, and as you said it was an extensive bombing operation that targeted alleged chemical weapons manufacturing facilities that were proven afterwards and also reported by OPCW to not be chemical weapons manufacturing facilities, brings into question the legality of that attack. It brings into question the legality of the entire regime change war that has been waged against Syria since 2011, of course instigated by those same nations that bombed after Douma.

But the fact that that the bombing went ahead without any OPCW investigation having been able to take place and based entirely on what is now proven or thought to be spurious information from groups like the White Helmets, that are being funded by the nations that carried out the bombing attack, I mean, this is an extraordinary event; this basically means that the US, the UK and France have completely violated international law time and time again inside Syria and this must be brought into the light, it must be investigated.

That is, alas, unlikely to happen, mainly because Britain has such a servile media. One is touched by Vanessa Beeley's concern for international law but it's doubtful whether UK politicians share her concern in this regard.

The *Pink Floyd's* lead guitarist Roger Waters has denounced the fake gas attack at Douma, asking the powers that bombed Damascus, 'How

do you sleep at night?' He described the story set up by the White Helmets as a 'callous and murderous fairytale.' "The White Helmets [may have] murdered 34 women and children to dress the scene that sorry day in Douma," he posted on his facebook page.[148]

Here is a tweet from US 'Real News' journalist Ben Norton, on how the UK-Government funded 'Integrity Initiative' was pushing the fake 'White Helmets' narrative in Syria.

The story of the bombing of Douma has grown into a thrilling, hyper-realistic 'Call of duty' wargame which has the player as an SAS and/or White Helmet member rescuing babies in Syria from deadly attacks by Russian planes - with Russian soldiers throwing nerve gas about! Not surprisingly, the Pentagon assisted in its creation. Our sanity is here rescued by blogger comments on its website 'Call of Duty: Al Qaeda Atrocity edition.' Eg, here is 'Josh 876': 'The blatant anti-Russian propaganda just confirms that the video game industry is already owned

148 See: stephenlendman.org/2019/12/new-evidence-of-opcw-doctored-douma-syria-report/ + off-guardian.org/2018/04/08/douma- chemical-attack-facts-so-far/ + discussion George Galloway and Syria Girl: dprogram.net/syrian-girl/the-mother-of-all-talkshows-syrian-girl-on-whats-happening-in-douma/ + Veterans Today denouncing the BBC for their pro-White Helmets position: veteranstoday.com/2021/04/20/fake-story-of-the-year-mossad-owned-news-outlet-ties-white-helmets-fake-chem-attack-whistleblowers-to-russia/

by "The Man" just like the rest of entertainment. And it isn't just geo-political propaganda, it is also the anti-White male stuff (feminism, anti-racism, anti Nationalism and all the usual crap).' Or, Pedro Vaz: 'What's with the Russian genocide happy soldiers? Which war is this supposed to represent/emulate, is it the Soviet Afghan war, because if not then that's one big fictional bullshittery.' Yang Gang: 'Since this game includes Russians in a ME country, "nerve gas" and the White Helmets aka Syria's "moderate" head choppers, presumably players will be able to behead Christians, stage fake gas attacks, rape and enslave Yazidis, and machine gun civilians then dump them into mass graves?' Josh 876[149]

'Yellow Rain' – how history repeats

We can make a comparison with a much earlier episode featuring alleged use of chemical weapons, drummed up by US/UK politicians for their nefarious purposes. Forty years ago, Porton Down laboratory was involved in an investigation of an alleged chemical weapon which turned out to be totally bogus and it was put into a dilemma quite comparable to what happened in the Skripal affair.

In 2018 World leaders were meeting together in Mid-March for a G7 summit comprising leaders of Canada, France, Germany, Italy, Japan, the United Kingdom, and the United States, Russia having been excluded. At that meeting on March 15th, the USA came round to accepting the British line concerning the Skripal story. Four of the nations (Germany, France, US and UK) put out a joint statement accusing Russia of having violated the 1925 Chemical Weapons Convention, where nations agreed to ban these dreadful weapons. The four nations brazenly asserted:

> This use of a military-grade nerve agent, of a type developed by Russia, constitutes the first offensive use of a nerve agent in Europe since the Second World War.

A day later I posted this riposte:

> No, you lying snakes, correction:

149 Charlieintel.com, 'Call of Duty: Modern Warfare Campaign Missions' 30.5.19

> This allegation of use of a military-grade nerve agent, is the first such fake-news accusing Russia of using nerve gas since 1982. The British government did indeed make this claim (in 1982, of 'Yellow Rain' in South-East Asia) then it turned out to be a natural substance from bees – the UK Government never apologized or retracted its untruthful accusation.[150]

Back in 1982, the world was poised for a major United Nations 'Special Session on Disarmament' and hopes ran high that it would put a cap on the nuclear arms race. However, the US President Ronald Reagan and the British Prime Minister Margaret Thatcher had a different agenda that involved starting up a new cold war, and so a diversion was needed. This duly arrived in the form of a shocking accusation that the Russians had been using poison gas in various parts of South-East Asia.

On the eve of that US Disarmament session, the 'Hague Report' (Al Hague was the US foreign Secretary) appeared, and it detailed what appeared to be a shocking story. 'Except to the wittingly obtuse, the evidence is conclusive' wrote the *Wall Street Journal*. The story was obscure, about complaints that had been emanating from Laos and Thailand. The accusation did indeed derail the United Nations disarmament conference, but was it true? The Soviets were shocked and bewildered, at being thus accused. A frightening book *Yellow Rain: A Journey through the terror of Chemical Warfare* appeared in 1982, followed by the more honest *The Yellow Rainmakers* of 1983 by the Australian Grant Evans. One of its last chapters, *Honest Delusion and Evil Propaganda,* should be mandatory reading for any civil servants who believed the Skripal story.

That alleged toxin was indeed – to cut a long story short - bee excrement. 'Yellow rain' was, it turned out, a natural phenomenon.[151] Though tortured logic and the jungles of South-East Asia, accounts of it had ended up in the weighty but delusional *Hague Report*. To its eternal credit, Britain's Porton Down establishment then refused to endorse the American story: it kept noticing that the samples of 'yellow rain' it was sent for analysis contained pollen! No doubt there is a moral here.

---

150 www.terroronthetube.co.uk 'UK Poison Hoax,' March 16.

151 'Is Yellow Rain Natural?' by Julian Perry Robinson, *World Armaments and Disarmament SIPRI Yearbook* 1984 pp.377-8, and 'Yellow Rain' SIPRI Yearbook 1985, pp.186-7.

Science is supposed to be a process of independent investigation, where any results the laboratories may come up with are *not* determined by whoever is paying them. Undue pressure from politicians is likely to make the process of scientific enquiry impossible. We the public may believe in some truth reported by a laboratory only if there is no arm-twisting going on, to confirm a pre-determined outcome.

A review of the 'Yellow Rain' debacle reflected that:

> The traditions of scientific enquiry, which place the utmost value on peer-review and on disclosure of sources and methods, do not sit comfortably into the heirarchical and secretive processes of government.[152]

That is really the crux of the matter. If, for example, different bio-labs had been allowed to analyse the content of that 'Novichok' perfume bottle (whether it existed is rather questionable however let's suppose for now that it did), and if furthermore they had compared this with various other samples found, then a conclusion could be reached, which would be a scientific judgment. There would be qualified bio-lab analysts doing what they were professionally trained to do, and a result that was reliable – and the OPCW would at last know what 'Novichok' was. Readers who have come this far will appreciate why none of that could be allowed to happen! Instead, political actors superimposed a *pre-determined* narrative, onto what was a mere *semblance* of scientific enquiry.

The scientific method should involve scientists who do *not* know the answer in advance, who *are* allowed to be sceptical, and who *can* disagree with one another. One may doubt whether these things were in fact the case for the lab workers at Porton Down - instead political pressures involving their future careers were applied, shrouded in secrecy.

On March 17th 2018 it was announced that Porton Down would be receiving £48 million to develop a brand-new Chemical Warfare Defence Centre. That was quick, a mere ten days after the event! It is hard to resist saying, that such sudden, massive funding greatly assists compliance with a pre-arranged agenda. It illustrates the simple principle, that those who collaborate in the process of state-fabricated terror, are the ones who benefit from it.

152 Julian Perry Robinson, 'Is Yellow Rain Natural?' SIPRI 1984, p.337.

Novichok in the High Court

The Inquest into the death of Dawn Sturgess at Amesbury, Wiltshire kept being postponed by the Wiltshire and Swindon County senior coroner David Ridley, because despite hundreds of police, military personell, forensic scientists and secret service agents, the Metropolitan Police found themselves unable to present a case for her cause of death. To this day no death certificate has been signed. Finally, on 30th March 2021 the case was transferred from Amesbury to the Royal Courts of Justice in London (dawnsturgessinquest.org.uk) .

The new 'final inquest' was to be being presided over by Lady Justice Hallett, the very same person who oversaw the 7/7 London bombings inquest back in 2011. She made some preliminary comments, and explained how she wanted the hearings to transition from being an Inquest into being an Enquiry- exactly as for the Litvinenko case years earlier! Then she announced she was resigning ... and so in 2022 the Enquiry is continuing with a new president! One could make a comparison here with the 7/7 London bombings Inquest of 2005 which Baroness Hallett likewise presided over and that too managed to make the subtle transition into being an Enquiry, and lasted for six months.

On March 30th at 11 am I endeavored to enter Britain's High Court on the Strand. 'We're closed, no public access' the doorman advised me – and indeed the enormous and majestic hall in front of me was totally empty: 'Coronavirus, y'know,' he added. I managed to persuade him to allow me entry then the lady at the enquiries desk could not find any record of the hearing under either 'Hallett' or 'Sturgess'. Finally she telephoned someone who could advise her and yes it was room 76. Passing through ancient stone corridors and winding staircases with gothic arches I finally arrived there, being not surprisingly the only member of the public to attend.

The proceedings have no counsel for the defence and no dissenting voice will question the government's narrative. Lady Justice Hallett was merely given one point of view, with no doubt being cast upon Russian guilt. Mr O'Connor, the barrister advising her in this hearing did however advise the court that the Russian embassy had posted a rebuttal of the UK's Skripal story and quoted briefly from it.[153]

The first day's hearing was replete with allusions to the Litvinenko case, where unproved Russian guilt had been 'strongly suspected.' As a predecessor and blueprint it seems to be vital for establishing the 'Let's blame Russia' mood.

Why would agents of the Russian state come to Wiltshire, LJH asked? Why indeed? She hoped to find out in this inquest /enquiry. Coroner Ridley in Amesbury had failed after repeated attempts to perform an Inquest, and so the highest British court in the land had to take up the matter.

The post-mortem on Sturgess carried out on July 17, 2018 unaccountably failed to result in a death certificate being signed. Wiltshire Senior Coroner David Ridley had earlier stated that no blood sampling of either Sturgess or Rowley at the hospital identified poisoning by a nerve agent; and that the hospital toxicology reports, also kept secret by the lawyers, identified criminal class-A drugs (heroin, methadone) in her blood.[154]

The purpose of an Inquest is to ascertain cause of death. A post-mortem report is therefore vital. The court was advised about the alleged contents of this in a written submission to the court, which curiously stated:

> On 17th July 2018, Professor Guy Rutty MBE, a Home Office Registered Forensic Pathologist conducted an independent post-mortem examination. He was accompanied by Dr Phillip Lumb, also an independent Home Office Registered Forensic Pathologist. Professor Rutty's Post-Mortem Report of 29th November 2018 records the cause of death as I.a, Post-cardiac arrest [leading to] hypoxic brain injury and intracerebral haemorrhage; I.b, Novichok

153 For transcript of proceedings, see Helmer's *Dances with Bears* 31 March 'First day shock at her majesty's government inquest Bellingcat to be called to testify but not Sergei or Yulia Skripal' where link is given.

154 Quoting from John Helmer 21.5.20, 'Skripal Showdown, Novichok Payday.' 'The Inquest touching upon the death of Dawn Kelly Sturgess, Case .no. 1380/18 Ridley 20.12.19.

toxicity.[155]

The two causes here given are quite incongruous. The first is what one would expect from a drug overdose: heart failure followed by 'brain injury.' She was brain-dead upon arriving at the hospital and what they kept on ventilation for a week was just a vegetable. A second and quite unconnected cause of death has been added: Novichok poisoning. If indeed that registered pathologist had put his name to such a report and such a sensational verdict; would it not have made newspaper headlines? If the post-mortem report 'did not follow' until four months later, November 29th, then the delayed inquest into Dawn Sturgess' death held a couple of months later in January 2019 would surely have used this as the centerpiece and the main press release? Instead that inquest was adjourned with no conclusion.

Figure: Dawn Sturgess

Lady Hallett wanted her remit to cover *who did it* which would involve hearing and re-evaluating the Skripal narrative. Thus, on July 24th 2018 Charlie Rowley had 'remembered' that the perfume bottle of Novichok he had found in a refuse bin had had an undamaged plastic wrapping – i.e., it was unopened. He had decided to give it as a present to his true love, with macabre consequences. After that, any theory of Russian guilt would require the two Russians who came over on March 3rd to Salisbury bringing with them *two* bottles of perfume containing Novichok, one of which was used to spray the Skripal's door-handle, and the other which was unused with the original shop plastic wrapping still intact, thrown into a park bin and remaining there for three months until found by Charlie Rowley. Then, the 'perfume bottle' which the police produced did not remotely resemble any actual Nino Ricci perfume bottle .. so how

155 Written submission of Counsel to the inquest for the Pre-Inquest hearing on 30 March 2021;' link in Helmer, 30.3.21.

could it have been in the undamaged 'Nino Ricci' wrapper?

Lady Hallett expressed a wish for the hearings to move at some point to Salisbury and or Amesbury. Would the two Skripals be called to testify? Those two have become unpersons, prisoners of the British government with no enquiries made as to their whereabouts. Unlike Alexei Navalny – who needed no encouragement to denounce Russia - they cannot be relied upon to give the required narrative and so have to remain silent. Yulia has after all stated that they would like to return to Russia.

Instead of calling the Skripals to testify, she declared the Inquest's intent to hear *Bellingcat* - described by John Helmer as 'the well-known NATO-funded evidence fabricator and cyber warfare unit'. Run by former underwear salesman Eliot Higgins, it enjoys close ties with US intelligence sources. How could *Bellingcat's* testimony be relevant to Dawn Sturgess' cause of death?

The highest concentrations of Novichok were found on the Skripals' front door handle, O'Connor advised LJH. But then, how about the police who arrived at the Skripals' house at 5 pm on the day of March 4th, 2018, seen happily going in and out of the house via the front door with none of them the worse for it? The story of Novichok-on-front-door story only appeared a few weeks later, long after the poison-in-the-Zizzi-restaurant story.

'Full disclosure,' a Secretary of State spokesperson (on a screen) advised the court, of the relevant Skripal material, could take two years. What was there left of the well-aired Skripal story to disclose that would take so long to dredge up?

A sensible comment here was posted by the Russian embassy, following the first day of the LJH Inquest:

> … the situation with regard to these tragic events [the Skripals' abduction] would evolve according to the Litvinenko Case scenario…The latest statement by the coroner indicates that she proceeds from an *a priori* belief that the two cases were interconnected, presumes responsibility of two Russian nationals for what happened to the Skripals and fully accepts the myths invented by the British secret services. We will now witness

> attempts to prove a case that has already been concocted beforehand.
>
> In the meantime, we have not yet received any requests for legal assistance from the British authorities. Nor is there any answer to the long list of our questions posed to them on multiple occasions in relation to what happened in Salisbury and what happens to Sergei and Yulia Skripal now.[156]

The chief legal advisor to LJH 'counsel to the Inquest' Andrew O'Connor QC was the security services representative in the Alexander Litvinenko inquiry, which seems appropriate.

Did Baroness Hallett fully comprehend the unhinged nature of the argument? She may have done after I sent her a four-page letter in November of 2021. I received a reply saying it had been much appreciated, soon after which her resignation was announced. She had told us much about what she was looking forward to doing with this Inquest – transitioning into an Enquiry and moving at some stage to Salisbury to hear the evidence: and now abruptly and without explanation she was gone. Years earlier, I had followed her Inquest/Enquiry into the London bombings of 2005 – and written it up in my *Terror on the Tube*, the (if I may say so) definitive book on the subject. It extended over six months in 2010/11, and there could not really be an Inquest because there had been *no post mortems.* That's right, no post-mortems on the 52 victims: so she subtly made the transition to an Enquiry so that the bad guys could be blamed. Muslims were then the enemy. It was Britain's major fabricated-terror event. But now here she was alas! bottling out …

The Enquiry is being continued by the little-known Lord Hughes. There would have to be, he explained at his first hearing in March of 2022, closed sessions in order to evaluate those aspects of the case which 'closely affect national security.' He revealed how the death of a drug-addict had *generated tens of thousands of documents*, as different police forces pooled their resources. He explained how 'the disclosure process' would gradually allow some fraction of these documents to be brought into the public domain and that would take a year or so. A lawyer

156 www.rusemb.org.uk/fnapr/6989

representing the Home Secretary assured the hearing that 'a large number of agencies and departments are reviewing the material.' The project is being called 'Operation Verbasco' with sixty counter-terror officers of Policing South East working hard on the case. They have checked though *twenty-two thousand documents* already, the Court was told, out of fifty thousand. John Helmer in his inimitable style has characterised these proceedings as: 'British Government's Novichok operation moves into new coverup stage.'

Wiltshire police are not involved in Operation Verbasco! For ascertaining the cause of death of Dawn Sturgess, you would not want Wiltshire police to be involved. I mean what do they know? Quite a lot, really. In fact too much, one could say. They have been warned: "To avoid any inadvertent disclosure of sensitive material, Wiltshire Police should adhere to the disclosure process developed by Operation Verbasco."[157] And '... the Operation Verbasco team are assisting Wiltshire Police in their disclosure process,' to make sure they keep in line.

Its clear that a lot of lawyers are making tidy sums of money from the millions of government money assigned to this Enquiry, which has transformed into a huge bureaucratic enterprise. It is growing so huge *because* it is untrue, having a core narrative of that which did *not* happen. The constant references to national security and the sensitivity of documents are indeed pertinent: the state has lied so badly and consistently that, for the truth to emerge would be a shattering event.

The Skripals we were told would be amongst the interested parties in the Enquiry, i.e. there would be a lawyer who represents them. They are designated as being amongst the 'core participants' in the Enquiry but that need not mean that they will appear or testify – if indeed they are still alive.

The mother of Sergei Skripal, Elena, passed away in January 2021, and every attempt was made to notify the Skripals in England. But, no word was heard from them – no flowers, no condolencies, nothing: "We can assume that they are not alive" reckoned Viktoria Skripal, because of that awful silence. It is therefore strange if they have now applied to participate in this Enquiry as Lord Hughes has indicated.

---

[157] Johnhelmer.net 13.12.21 'Novichok operation moves into new coverup stage'.

Part III:

THE FATE OF ALEXEI NAVALNY

Navalny was *built* (italics mine) by the usual suspects as a battering ram to undermine Nord Stream 2.

- Pepe Escobar

'Novichok' Strikes Again

The Salisbury Novichok hoax had worked so well in creating a wave of anti-Russian hysteria - over 150 Russian diplomats expelled when only the cat had died – so, why not try it again? The looming event was the completion of the nearly-finished Nord Stream II gas pipeline from Russia to Germany, the world's longest-ever pipeline, in 2020. It was a matter of supreme importance for the Empire, that this project be cancelled. Were it to be completed and start to function, there would be a real danger of world peace breaking out. Nothing could be more valuable for the stability of the world, than a slowly growing trust and friendship between the two great nations of Germany and Russia. These two nations have both been heavily demonised by the US/UK in the past, in the 20th century. A reliable flow of natural gas in a stable manner between the two nations would have more effect than the words of politicians.

Instead of spending trillions on NATO military hardware, with US

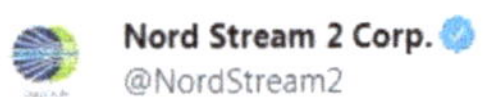

More than 1,000 companies from 25 different countries are involved in the
construction of the Nord Stream 2 Pipeline, such as Europipe in Mühlheim,
Germany, where much of the pipe was produced:
bit.ly/31n9GbX

weapons being moved ever closer to the borders of Russia threatening war, European nations could slowly come to experience Russia as a valuable trading partner. Instead of Germany having US and British troops permanently stationed there and continually rehearsing war-games, as if WW2 had hardly ended, Germany would be able to become a more pacific and independent nation, able to determine its own future without foreign military occupation.

Germany is endeavoring to move away from its reliance upon nuclear power and fossil fuels, and that might only be possible with such a pipeline. And yet the EU parliament has *instructed* Germany to abandon the project – with the implication that it would instead buy the far more expensive US 'freedom gas' that comes from fracking! Germany as an industrial nation depends upon its industries having a reputation for reliability and adherence to promises. It may have the best science and technology in the world, but for its industry to flourish it also needs a reputation for dependability. That is not acquired overnight but takes years, as clients come to reckon that in fact German firms will deliver as promised. And yet Germany is has been told by the EU to break and abandon contracts with around a hundred different companies (it is estimated) who have laboured to complete the pipeline. How would that affect Germany's hard-won reputation in the field of commerce? One thing's for sure: the voices calling for Germany to abandon the pipeline project do not care!

A subtle and very clever hoax was perpetrated involving the poisoning of Alexei Navalny. We'll analyse it here by making comparisons with the UK's Skripal hoax.

<u>Figure:</u> Navalny before the event

Alexei Navalny has done no doubt excellent and much-needed work in exposing corruption and graft in Russia with his 'Anti-Corruption Foundation' (the 'FKB'). He is well-funded by Western sources and in 2010 was awarded a Yale Scholarship, i.e he is regarded as a politically useful tool of the US. As the most prominent Russian dissident, his weekly videos can receive over ten million views, as they expose the way politicians have been siphoning off what should be public funds for private profit. Readers may wish to view one or two of his entertaining and quite shocking videos, to get a sense of what is involved.[158]

We can all imagine a *story*, whereby agents of the Russian state would endeavor to remove him, as being a prominent thorn in the side of the government. However, under the current circumstances, would that be credible? Would it not sound rather like a contrived narrative, that his eminence and notoriety be used by those who wish to discredit Russia?

August 20th

Navalny and his aides had been working in the Siberian town of Tomsk, to try and persuade the locals as regards how they should vote in an upcoming election. Early in the morning of August 20th, Navalny leaves his room in the Xander hotel with a taxi waiting for him, accompanied by two of his aides. Then he gets a bus for a thirty-minute ride to the airport. Some on the bus recognize him, and comment on how he looks fine and cracks jokes.[159]

His flight to Moscow takes off at 7.50 am. Half an hour after take-off he collapses in the aisle of the plane. Five minutes later the plane decides to re-route and its pilot applies to make an emergency landing at the nearby Omsk airport because they have a hospital there.

Before landing and five minutes after that request for an emergency landing, the local police at Omsk receive a bomb threat: 'bombs in the out-building' which led to immediate evacuation of the airport terminal. That is a very interesting synchrony. However it does not prevent the brave hospital emergency staff from boarding the plane. They see Navalny in a coma and they are puzzled to note that his two companions do not seem surprised, and later comment: 'It is as if they knew what is about to happen.' Soon after this, one of his two aides tweets 'Alexei has

---

158 Eg, youtube.com/watch?v=nMVJxTcU8Kg - Prime Minister Medvedev's huge stately home.

159 Vesti News: 'Navalny Fake poisoning Exclusive' 24.8.21

toxic poisoning.' That was the first mention of this concept, which would rapidly spread worldwide *that very day*. Quickly he was taken to the hospital where dangerously low blood sugar levels were found, and he was put on a ventilator. They probably save his life. He's given a small amount of atropine.

We're then told that his other aides in Tomsk who were just having breakfast quickly go to his hotel room. They video record themselves doing this, wearing sterile gloves with Maria Pevchikh seen co-ordinating things. They collect two or three half-litre bottles of mineral water. Are they not here *creating* a story? Would Navalny really have left more than one bottle of half-drunk water? The video shows her wearing a Rolex watch in the video – as John Helmer noticed[160] - and a close-up enlargement showed its time at between 9 and 9.30 am. One other worker has a watch and again enlargement showed it reading a time of around 9 O'clock.

There is a one-hour time-difference between Tomsk time and that of Omsk where the plane landed. Using the Tomsk timezone, the tweet alleging his poisoning would have gone out around 8.40 am. For the three aides then to be filming each other in his Xander Hotel bedroom with sterile gloves etc. hardly seems possible a mere half an hour later: that has to be either a pre-arranged event or filmed much later. We bear in mind here that nobody heard a word about these water bottles being collected before September 17th, as we'll see. Also when Pevchikh went through the checkout for her air flight that morning to join Navalny, she had no water bottles in her suitcase! (The transport police released an X-ray of it). If this whole story was retro-constructed it would help to account for the deep silence of the Xander Hotel who probably knew very well that no collection of left-behind water bottles had happened that morning.

To continue with the narrative, the Boeing 737 passenger flight S7 2614 airline Tomsk to Moscow made its flight diversion at 9.10, Omsk time. After Navalny had collapsed in the aisle, at 9.18 the flight diverted to Omsk, and by 9.50 it had dropped to an altitude at which mobile phones could work. It landed at 9.56 am.[161]

One would like further analysis of these timings by some Russians, but

---

160 Helmer, *Dances with Bears* 21.9.20 'Navalny, Pevchikh are barking dogs'

161 www.fagain.co.uk/node/67 Omsk time is one hour behind = 8.56.

for now let's merely say that if indeed mobile phones on the plane could not function prior to 9.50 (8.50 am Omsk time) then that would make the morning bottle-collection even more impossible.

Pevchikh drives to Novobirsk aiport and then carries no bottles of water through customs (we'll later see how she allegedly carries 'the bottle' to Germany for analysis). She is seen buying a similar half-litre water bottle at that airport prior to boarding.

Many newspaper headlines start to appear that evening and both Angela Merkel and Emmanuel Macron make statements that their country is willing to receive the patient. This is looking rather pre-prepared.

August 21: A mystery German 'ambulance plane' lands at Omsk airport and waits, desiring to transport the comatose patient to Berlin. The hospital does not agree. Navalny aides then 'denounced the medical verdict as a ploy to stall until any poison would no longer be found in his body.' The claim of poisoning is made at Omsk, despite doctors at the hospital failing to confirm it. It was alleged that the poison had come from tea he had drunk at the Tomsk airport in Siberia.

August 22: he is flown to Germany for treatment.

August 24: German doctors declare that they found signs of Navalny's intoxication with substances from the cholinesterase inhibitors group.

September 2: the German Government issued a press release, saying 'a special Bundeswehr laboratory carried out a toxicological test using samples from Alexej Nawalny. Thereby the unequivocal proof of a chemical nerve warfare agent of the Novichok group was provided.'

September 3: the UK government said that there was 'unequivocal proof' that the Russian had been poisoned. The EU issued a declaration stating: 'The EU strongly condemns the assassination attempt of Alexei Navalny, calls for a joint international response & reserves the right to take appropriate actions.'

September 4: ambassadors of NATO member states decide to convene a "special meeting" in Brussels.

September 6: OPCW comes to Berlin and takes blood samples from Navalny.

September 9: German Defence Ministry announces that the results of the testing of Navalny's blood and urine, plus a water bottle which had been brought to Berlin at the same time as Navalny, would not be handed to the Russian Government, as it has been requesting.

September 10: Angela Merkel accuses Russia of poisoning and threatens sanctioning of the Nord Stream II gas pipeline

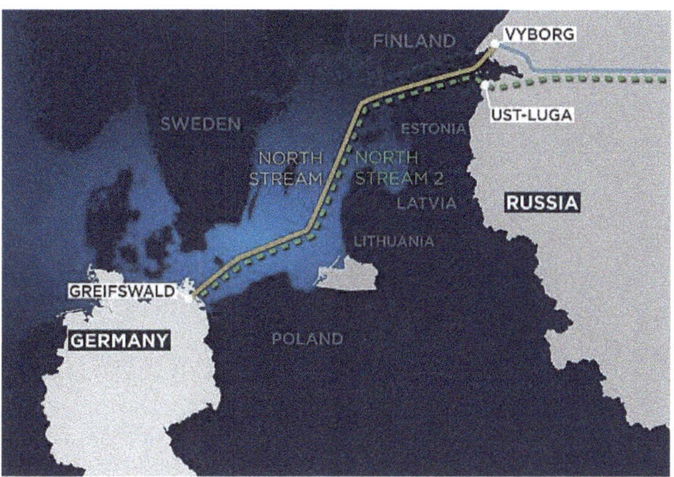

Figure: The Nordstream-II pipeline, destined not to function?

September 14: France backs up poison claim: 'French President Emmanuel Macron's office said he had expressed "deep concern over the criminal act" that targeted Navalny.'

September 15: Navalny emerges from his coma.

September 17: EU Parliament expresses ' … utmost concern about the repeated use of chemical nerve agents against Russian citizens' and calls for halting of the Nord Stream II project.

Film of Navalny aides collecting bottles in Xander hotel room released. The claim is first made, that they contained the Novichok poison.

October 6: OPCW declared that Navalny's blood contained a 'cholinesterase inhibitor' that was 'not listed in the Annex on Chemicals to the Convention' - ie not a recognized poison. They did not as such confirm the presence of Novichok.

October 15th: The EU agrees to impose sanctions on six Russian officials, allegedly involved in the poisoning.

Figure: Navalny recovering from 'Novichok' with his wife who is holding a mask

Problems arose with this narrative: could the poison really work so slowly, that only many hours after allegedly taking it, Navalny would fall unconscious? Could he really succumb to a deadly nerve poison even though no-one else around him was infected? For comparison, the Skripal story originally had the couple poisoned in a restaurant, then when that appeared too unlikely the poison was alleged to have been in their home – similarly creating a several-hour interval between the alleged poisoning and its sudden effect. The parallels between the two stories may lead one to suspect the same scriptwriter.

Since his recovery, Navalny has been promoting the view that President Putin wanted to kill him. But, would the Russian state really wish to commit an assassination so very publicly, one that would instantly generate a vast international condemnation? Would it moreover decide to use 'Novichok' to poison him, in spite of the facts that a) Novichok had dramatically failed to work in their alleged attempted murder of the Skripals and b) It has already been widely publicly associated with Russia? None of that would make sense.

To no-one's surprise, the Novichok which didn't kill its alleged target last time, doesn't kill its alleged target this time either. It has to be the least effective assassination tool ever! It left both its supposed victims in a state of unconsciousness for almost exactly the same period of days. Navalny remained unconscious for 26 days as likewise Yulia Skripal, two years earlier, had stayed under for 25 days. As Julia Skripal was soon seen alive and well after her poisoning, looking younger and more debonair than before - so likewise we soon see pictures of Navalny recovered and nonchalantly strolling around!

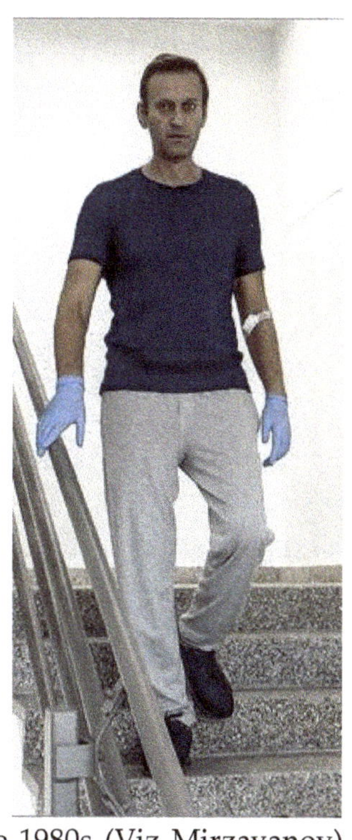

He emerged quite slowly from his coma. At first he could hardly find words: 'Although I understood in general what the doctor wanted, I did not understand where to get the words. What part of the head do they appear in? I also did not know how to express my despair and therefore, simply kept silent. Now I'm a guy whose legs are shaking when he walks up the stairs, but he thinks, 'Oh, this is a staircase! They go up it.'[162] He evidently has no idea who has done what to him and so blames the Kremlin. He told his story to a *New Yorker* journalist, of how he suffered at the hands of his wicked government.[163] It merited a couple of sceptical and scornful comments shown here.

His story greatly lacks credibility - for a start he never displayed any Novichok-type symptoms. A Soviet researcher who had been involved in developing Novichok back in the 1980s (Viz Mirzayanov) explained the symptoms on a BBC program: they start with sudden blindness, followed by difficulty breathing, then constant vomiting and 'uncontrollable convulsions.' None of this happened to Navalny, when he fell into a coma. It causes lasting nerve damage and it's effects are immediate, they don't wait for several hours. Another chemical-weapons expert stated, "I believe that the use of chemical warfare substances sarin, soman and Novichok (A-234) can be excluded from the list of possibilities. Apart from Navalny himself, the people around him would be also stricken in one form or another.[164]

162 20 Sept. newseu: 'Navalny now able to walk and talk after coma.'
163 'Alexey Navalny Has the Proof of His Poisoning' By Masha Gessen, *The New Yorker* 19.10.20
164 Helmer Op. Cit. p156; RT 2.1020, 'Developers of 'Novichok' say Navalny's symptoms aren't consistent with poisoning by their deadly creation.'

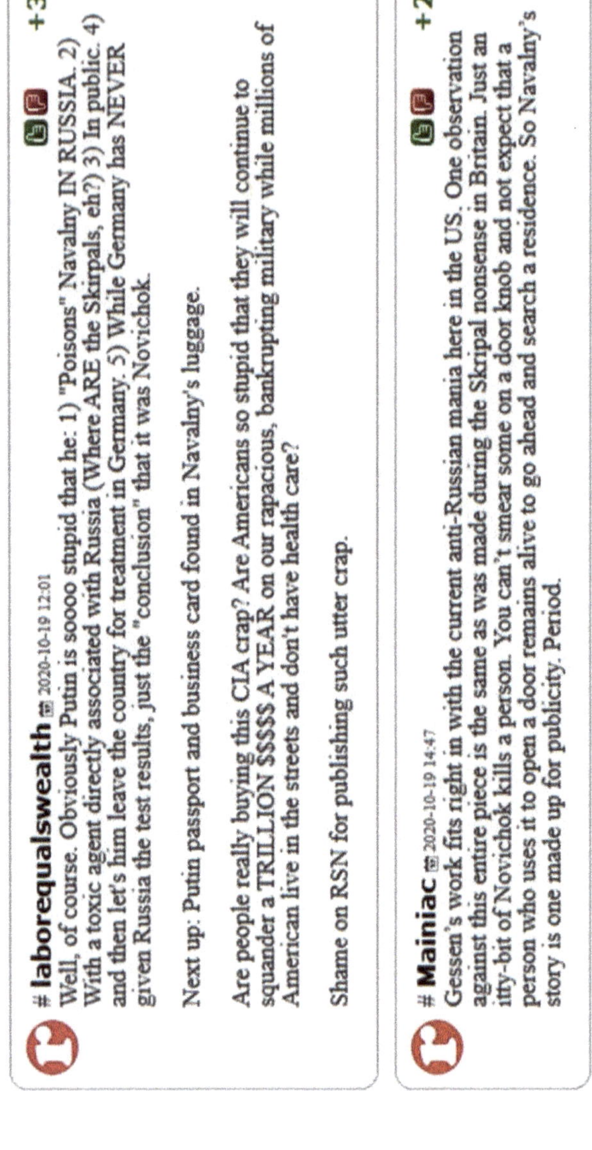

laborequalswealth 2020-10-19 12:01 +3

Well, of course. Obviously Putin is soooo stupid that he: 1) "Poisons" Navalny IN RUSSIA. 2) With a toxic agent directly associated with Russia (Where ARE the Skirpals, eh?) 3) In public. 4) and then let's him leave the country for treatment in Germany. 5) While Germany has NEVER given Russia the test results, just the "conclusion" that it was Novichok.

Next up: Putin passport and business card found in Navalny's luggage.

Are people really buying this CIA crap? Are Americans so stupid that they will continue to squander a TRILLION $$$$ A YEAR on our rapacious, bankrupting military while millions of American live in the streets and don't have health care?

Shame on RSN for publishing such utter crap.

Mainiac 2020-10-19 14:47 +2

Gessen's work fits right in with the current anti-Russian mania here in the US. One observation against this entire piece is the same as was made during the Skripal nonsense in Britain. Just an itty-bit of Novichok kills a person. You can't smear some on a door knob and not expect that a person who uses it to open a door remains alive to go ahead and search a residence. So Navalny's story is one made up for publicity. Period.

Figure: two sceptical and scornful comments.

The initial story of him being poisoned from a cup of tea at the airport lasted for several weeks, but then it morphed into a left-behind bottle of water in his hotel room. Don't even ask where that bottle of water is or who has got it – it is as invisible and forever-unseeable as was the perfume bottle allegedly brought over by the two Russians who were said to have poisoned the Skripals. No CCTV exists to show him drinking from the bottles or having it with him. The later water-bottle story had the advantage of supplying a sample of the deadly 'Novichok,' that could allegedly be matched up with what they found in Navalny.

Marina Pevchikh

Marina Pevchikh was described by the *Daily Mail* as the 'glamorous UK-based Navalny employee, 33' (17 Sept.) and by the satirical Russian column, 'Skripal's Cat' as '"Agent MI-6" Maria Pevchikh on high heels.'[165]

Living in London, she would travel to Moscow several times a year. There are not many photos of her, despite her being a close associate of Navalny, aged 44. Putting her name in Google brings up images of her with Navalny looking as if she were close to him (NB, I re-checked this on 30th September and these had gone, in fact almost all images of her are gone and one is merely shown images of Mr Navalny). Her father Konstanin Pevchikh is the head and founder of *several biological labs* (!).

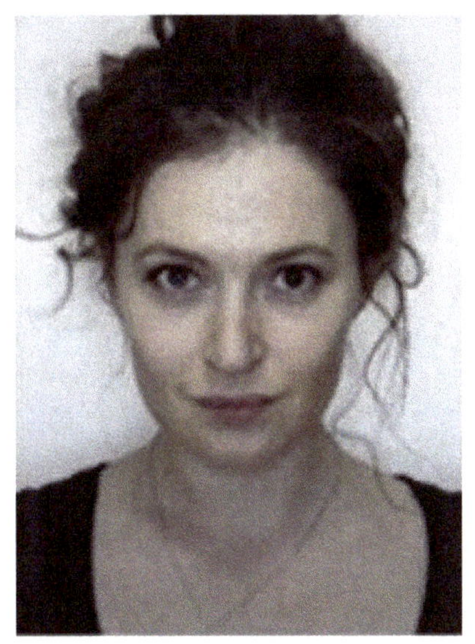

Figures: images of the elusive Ms. Pevchikh, the second as featured in *Daily Mail.* Are they the same person?

She acquired a degree in sociology from Moscow State University then later graduated in political science at the London School of Economics. Her record in the UK reveals a working association with anti-Russian regime-change organizations. Here are some Russian comments about her:

165 https://vz.ru/opinions/2020/9/20/1061378.html I have put English translations of the 'Skripal's Cat' articles on terronthetube.co.uk.

'She accompanied Navalny very closely during his stay in Siberia and spent the nights in his hotel room. She has tight connections to the Russian oligarch Khodorkovsky, who lives in the UK and to Vladimir Ashurkov, who is the head of Navalny's bureau against corruption.' (RT blog comment).

German officials refused to comment upon this close associate of Navalny. The associate of the Kremlin critic was reportedly together with Navalny in Tomsk before his alleged poisoning. Unlike all other individuals who interacted with him on that day, she did not cooperate with Russian investigators and quickly left the country for Germany.

How did a Russian citizen manage to obtain a permit for entering the country so fast, especially with Covid-19 restrictions supposedly in place? Little is actually known about Pevchikh, who is believed to hold a UK residence permit – or even citizenship. Moreover, only a few photos of her exist, despite her close association and repeated trips alongside Navalny, who is a very public figure.

Comments about the Navalny affair tend to omit mention of this woman, although she has to be *the* link to British intelligence, relevant in view of the many similarities to the Skripal affair. Author John Helmer earlier wrote the book *Skripal in Prison* about the British Novichok hoax two years earlier, so he is well-qualified to evaluate this matter. Quoting from him:

'This evidence - the only evidence available to the Munich laboratory, and then to the French and Swedish labs – was the bottle which had been brought to Berlin with Navalny, carried either by his wife Yulia Navalnaya or by the witness who was with him in Tomsk and is the only one of the six staff from Tomsk to have accompanied him on the aircraft to Berlin. That is Maria Pevchikh.

This evidence lacks the required chain of custody for prosecution of a crime in a court of law. Also, the bottle and Pevchikh appear to have disappeared. Pevchikh left the alleged crime scene after spending the night with Navalny in Tomsk. As he flew towards Moscow, Pevchikh drove to Novosibirsk. She then flew to Omsk where Navalny's flight had been diverted and he was hospitalised. On August 22 Pevchikh was aboard the charter flight with Navalny from Omsk to Berlin, and then arrived at the Charité Hospital with his wife Yulia Navalnaya.

Pevchikh appears to have left Germany and is now in the UK. Every other witness, including five of Navalny's staff who had been with him in Tomsk, have been interviewed by police in Russia, and they are talking freely to the Russian and western press. Russian Foreign Minister Sergei Lavrov said on state television: "we questioned those five people who accompanied him to the plane, and took part in the events of the days before Navalny boarded the plane. We posed questions to those who waited for the departure from Tomsk to Moscow and went to a bar with him. We found out what they ordered and what he drank. As you know, the sixth lady that accompanied him just fled. They say it was she who gave the bottle to the German laboratory. All this was done. Even if all this were called a 'criminal case', we cannot do anything else." (Monday 13th September)

The "sixth lady" is Pevchikh. Her record in the UK reveals her working association with anti-Russian regime-change organisations of Yevgeny Chichvarkin, Mikhail Khodorkovsky, and Navalny's Anti-Corruption Foundation; Navalny's staff claim Pevchikh has been employed as head of investigations for their group.[166]

The plastic bottle of drinking water was not presented at the Omsk hospital, but was taken on the private jet charter flight with Navalny to Berlin on August 22. Ms Pevchikh and Navalny's wife reportedly had 'the bottle.' At Berlin, they arrived in the airport motorcade at the clinic.

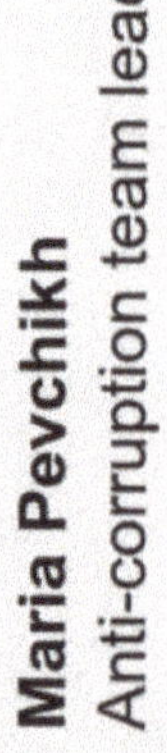

One bottle had microscopic traces of Novichok on it - the same agent which was found in Alexei's body by three independent laboratories
Maria Pevchikh
Anti-corruption team leader

Russia should ask for the extradition of Maria Pevchikh. She was crucially involved in whatever happened to Navalny to make him fall unconscious, and central in constructing a fake narrative about getting bottles of water from the Xander hotel in Tomsk. The whole thing looks suspiciously pre-planned and interrogating her about what happened that morning could help to resolve this. She vanished after playing her part and returned to London; but then on 17th of September, as the water-bottle story was released, she gave an interview with the BBC. Later she put in a brief appearance in February of 2021, tweeting about the 'Putin's Palace' story.

166 www.sott.net/article/441422-The-Pevchikh-plot-Navalnys-bottle-London-witness-flees-scene-of-crime-and-Berlin-too.

Did he drink Poison?

On August 23rd when Navalny had been moved to a Berlin hospital, the media were putting out the cup-of-tea-at-the-airport story: he is 'feared to have drunk tea laced with poison' and then later "His supporters suspect he was poisoned when he drank a cup of tea at Tomsk Airport in Siberia on August 20." (Mail 23rd and 29th) If they were suspecting the cup of tea, why would they have rushed to the hotel?

A report by the *American Association for the Advancement of Science* for 8th September has him poisoned by 'drinking a cup of tea at a Siberian airport.'[167] On September 10th the *Mail* explained that this was a *yet more deadly* form of Novichok, which someone at the airport had slipped into his tea – while surrounded by half a dozen of his aides! But then, Russian CCTV at the airport proved that his airport cup of tea could not have been poisoned.

On September 17th ie *almost a month after the event,* the cup of tea story vanished from media sources and instead the source of poison became a plastic bottle of water. A video appeared showing members of his team searching the room he had just left in the Xander Hotel in Tomsk on August 20 – being directed by Marina Pevchikh[168] - and finding three left-behind bottles of water.

She was wearing a Rolex watch in the video – as John Helmer noticed - and a close-up enlargement showed its time at between 9 and 9.30 am. One other worker has a watch and again enlargement showed it reading a time of around 9 O'clock. On that morning, Navalny's plane which took off at 7.55 am would still have been in the air.[169] That is long before any poisoning had been alleged and *indicates a staged event.*

That Boeing 737 passenger plane (flight SB12614) airline Tomsk to Moscow had to make a flight diversion: at 9.10 Navalny started feeling unwell and collapsed in the aisle, then at 9.18 the flight diverted to Omsk,

167 www.sciencemag.org/news/2020/09/how-german-military-scientists-likely-identified-nerve-agent-used-attack-alexei-navalny

168 As pointed out by John Helmer: http://johnhelmer.net/navalny-pevchikh-are-barking-dogs-merkel-and-nord-stream-2-are-the-caravan-which-moves-on/

169 Ibid. The Tomsk timezone is 7 hours ahead of GMT.

and by 9.50 it had dropped to an altitude at which mobile phones could work. It landed at 9.56 am.[170]

There is a severe temporal dislocation in this story. Any Navalny supporters could not possibly have heard about his collapse prior to 9.50 am. The video of them collecting the water bottles from the hotel room cannot be genuine.

Why would they at once collect several water bottles using sterile gloves, and then take these bottles all the way to Berlin on the 22nd - and if so, how come the world was still being told the poisoned cup of tea story for several weeks after that? What would his team be doing at the hotel if they believed he had been poisoned at the airport? Will the hotel confirm that they had not attempted to tidy up the just-vacated room, and that several partly-drunk water bottles were left behind?

The 'Navalny team' put out their statement on 17th September that several bottles of water had been recovered from the Xander Hotel where he stayed in Tomsk, Siberia, and that using gloves they had carefully put the bottles into paper bags for transport. 'We drove to Novosibirsk and flew to Omsk from there' explained Ms Pevchikh.[171]

On this 'final' version of the story (17th September) the water bottles were *empty*, and the Novichok on the *outside* of them! The news headline became 'Navalny aides say nerve agent was found on hotel water bottle.' Quoting from a couple of pro-Navalny Russian media outlets, *Meduza* and *Proekt*,[172] the *Meduza* '… reached out to Maria Pevihikh, who leads the investigative department of Navalny's Anti-Corruption Foundation (the FBK). She accompanied Navalny on his trip to Siberia and was with him in Tomsk.' From her they gathered that she (or Navalny's aides) had taken three empty water bottles, which Navalny drank from, from his hotel room. *Proekt's* investigation says the poison was found *on* the bottle rather than in the water itself. These empty bottles had been transported to Berlin. On this version he absorbed the toxin though his hands – which no hospital has suggested. But the final OPCW report on October 6th did not endorse the water-bottle story: samples were *only* analysed from his

170 www.fagain.co.uk/node/67 Omsk time is one hour behind = 8.56.
171 BBC News 23 Sept. Navalny: 'How his team found Novichok bottle'
172https://meduza.io/en/feature/2020/09/17/navalny-s-team-reveals-hotel-room-search-that-uncovered-water-bottle-with-traces-of-Novichok-type-poison

blood and urine.

Had the phantom assassin entered his bedroom in the night, placing this poisoned bottle with such cunning that when Navalny woke up in the morning and even though it had not been there the night before, he would pick it up and drink it?

Both the cup of tea and the bottle of water stories had to be abandoned when it was pointed out that the effects of drinking any such potion would have been instantaneous. There were some who reckoned that merely touching a surface contaminated in this way could have a delayed effect on the victim, several hours later. So we end up with the mad story of his aides finding abandoned water bottles with Novichok on the *outside*. How could the ghostly hand of some Russian agent have placed them inside his hotel room and how could his aides have collected them without becoming contaminated themselves?

It seems that Pevchikh and one other Navalny aide did travel from Tomsk to Novosibirsk by car that morning and then to Omsk by plane. However, security at Novosibirsk airport have confirmed that they did *not* find such bottles in their luggage. On October 8th Mr Popatov, the 'Interior Ministry Deputy Director of the Investigative Department of the Transport Department for the Siberian Federal District' stated[173]:

> As Marina Pevchikh went through pre-flight checks in Tolmachevo (Novosibirsk) Airport, her suitcase and backpack did not have any liquid containers of over 100 milliliters, including any bottles of water.

So, she lied. They weren't carrying bottles of water.

If the Navalny team or some of them have fabricated parts of this story, *as they clearly have,* then they become *de facto* the chief suspects.

In November the matter was discussed in the German parliament, the *Bundestag*, when a Government spokesman had to answer questions put by representatives of AfD, the Alternative for Germany party. Here's an excerpt of some of the answers – or rather, the stonewalling whereby answers were avoided - published on November 19th:

Q62. How is it possible that Maria Pevichkh was able to bring a highly

173 8 Oct. RT, 'Siberian investigators dispute claims that Navalny's team transported Novichok-laced water bottle to Berlin.'

> toxic substance from Tomsk via Omsk to Berlin without putting herself and others at serious risk?
> A: The Federal Government has no knowledge of this.
>
> Q64. Did the Federal Government organize an analysis of whether when Alexei Navalny came into contact with a poisoned water bottle, the traces of Novichok should have been found on Navalny's hands, and his fingerprints should have been found on the bottle itself?
> A: The Federal Government has no findings on the question of fingerprints.
>
> Q65. Has the Federal Government taken steps to ensure the water bottle was checked for all fingerprints? If so, what were the results and whose prints were found? If not, why not?
> A: It is not the responsibility of the Federal Government to conduct a forensic examination
>
> Q75. Has the Federal Government released the exact composition of the Novichok compound found? If not, why not?
> A: Given the high risks of the leaking of information, the Federal Government did not disclose [to the Russian government] any details of the substance used."[174]

Only four questions are selected here of the many that were asked. One senses the way in which, not being a sovereign nation – still occupied since WW2 - Germany is obliged to toe the NATO line. The bottles of water remained a topic of discussion for several months, forming the basis for the Russian guilt accusation - after which they too vanished down the memory-hole.

The claim of Novichok poisoning only appeared when Navalny was in Germany and two weeks after the incident. The August 24th report which came from the Berlin Charité Hospital ('poisoning by a substance from the group of cholinesterase inhibitors') was merely signed by a press agent, not a doctor or head of the patient treatment team, as is required by German hospital protocol. That press agent was called Manuiela Zingl and when asked she refused to provide details of the head of Navalny's treatment team or of the treatment he had received. For an undisclosed reason, further research on Navalny was then conducted at the German

174 Johnhelmer.net, 'Plan revealed in Bundestag for Navalny Novichok operation' 2.2.20

army's chemical warfare laboratory in Munich, the IPTB.

On September 2nd, Angela Merkel's spokesman Steffen Seibert, stated that analysis of the bottle evidence by the *Institut für Pharmakologie und Toxikologie der Bundeswehr* had been reported to Merkel and a meeting of her ministers: "on this occasion, the definite proof [*zweifelsfreie Nachweis*] of a chemical nerve agent of the Novitchok (sic) group was produced."[175] This was a brief report with no details of any toxicology analysis, nor even the name of the IPTB expert in charge.[176]

In view of subsequent developments, we note that Navalny's wife Yulia Navalnaya claimed to have brought all of her husband's clothes to Berlin together with the bottle of water. She wrested a suitcase of Navalny's clothes away from the local police at the Omsk airport to take it on board the charter flight to Berlin.

Let's Blame Russia!

If Russians were intending to kill him, would the plane he was in really have performed an emergency landing so that Navalny could be taken straight to a hospital for medical care? Would they really have allowed a German plane to land at Omsk and wait there at the airport while he was being treated in the hospital and would they have yielded to his friends' demands to let him be flown to Berlin?

At a time when when there was no air communication between Russia and Germany due to the coronavirus pandemic, how was it possible for him to be suddenly flown out? 'Are the skies closed for all except Navalny,' people wondered? This was some high-level operation!

A policy of non-collaboration was swiftly decided upon by the German Defence Ministry:

> On Wednesday, [10th September] the German Defence Ministry announced that the results of the testing of Navalny's blood and

175 Helmer, Dances with Bears, 'Navalny story collapses in self-contradiction' 8.10.20; also, 'Brain poisoning with Russian nerve agent, Alexei Navalny infects German Chancellery.' 6.9.20

176 *Unz.com* 21.3.21 John Ryan, 'The Case of Alexei Navalny'

urine, plus a water bottle which had appeared in Berlin at the same time as Navalny, would not be handed to the Russian Government as it has been requesting. The results had been prepared by the Defence Ministry's chemical warfare laboratory in Munich, the *Institut für Pharmakologie und Toxikologie der Bundeswehr* (IPTB), and announced on Sept. 2nd.[177]

Had they found the same toxin in the bottled water as in his blood? The analysis was done by NATO medics in a chemical warfare laboratory! This has to remind us of Porton Down, Britain's Bio-warfare centre, doing the Skripal blood-analysis of the 'Novichok' - where it was widely believed that they were far more likely to have *supplied* the Novichok than *detected* it.

Analysis of Navalny's blood and urine by the Russian medics had indicated that his coma was likely introduced by a diabetes condition of low blood sugar. The Omsk Hospital report concluded, "cholinesterase inhibitors were not detected in blood and urine" and that meant, no 'Novichok.'

By this time Russia had grown sceptical of the NATO-EU narrative and they asked -

> Why was Mr. Navalny upon his arrival to Berlin escorted to the Charité Hospital by police and special service agents? Why were extraordinary security measures taken and the hospital itself turned into a high-security facility, well before the "discovery" of "Novichok"? Does it mean that Berlin knew something that neither Moscow nor Omsk were aware of? It is worth noting that more than 60 biochemical tests were conducted in the Omsk Hospital, none showing any sign of poisoning.
>
> What is behind the story of the "bottle of water", ostensibly with traces of poison on it? No CCTV or photo evidence shows Mr. Navalny using it before departure at Tomsk airport. If used before that or aboard the Moscow-bound plane, how did it get to Berlin? [178]

177 www.sott.net/article/441312-Germans-now-claim-God-poisoned-Navalny-thats-the-god-out-of-the-machine

178 https://russiaeu.ru/printpage/en/node/4489 'Comments on the situation with Alexey Navalny' 15 Sept.

Those are good questions and they might well point to a pre-prepared plot with military personnel taking over a Berlin hospital. We are reminded here of the British army's chemical-biological warfare war-games on Salisbury plain that *synchronised with* the Skripal story. Pictures of bottles of half-drunk water in a hotel room were released, where Navalny had slept before his flight. Before the plane had even landed, and before the hospital had not even sought for any signs of poisoning, did the colleagues of Navalny very suddenly decide to seek for signs of his having been poisoned? Would they not have assumed that the hotel cleaners had tidied up that vacant room?

The Berlin Charité Hospital's press release was dated August 24 and *un*signed by a treating doctor or toxicologist. It claimed "clinical findings indicate poisoning with a substance from the group of cholinesterase inhibitors. The specific substance involved remains unknown". The physicians involved remain anonymous and the *Bundeswehr* biochemical warfare lab that delivered the diagnosis refused to release a detailed report on how it analyzed the samples.

Throughout this whole affair Russia is the one country involved which has preserved customary principles of diplomacy. It seems to be the one country whose spokespersons are worth listening to because they still aspire to integrity and honesty in their speech; this is in itself a very strange situation. Here is what the Russian Foreign Secretary Lavrov stated on 11th September, in his usual polite fashion:

> We are interested in receiving, if not directly, then through the OPCW, information that Germany is for some reason so painstakingly concealing.[179]

One may readily understand why Germany could not allow the sharing of its bio-medical analysis of the Navalny blood/urine tests. Russians would want to ascertain as to whether they had really received 'water bottles' and if so when, and what was found on them? As the water bottle story only appeared several weeks after the event, the German authorities would not be in a hurry to answer that. American firms produced and patented several kinds of 'Novichok' in 2015 – whereas Russia is on record as having destroyed their bio-warfare stocks – and so the Russians would have wanted to compare the Novichok

179 https://www.rusemb.org.uk/article/646

found with these examples above.

Germany is thus violating the terms of the Chemical Weapons Convention (Article VII) by refusing to share its data with Russia.

Traditionally the home of philosophy, Germany had long enjoyed a certain reputation for honesty amongst its politicians, now evidently gone. Was it so easy for them to be manipulated, after a little arm-twisting by shadowy Atlanticists? What could be more evanescent and groundless than the bottle of water story? Obviously it quickly vanished – together with the elusive Maria Pevchikh.

Navalny accused the Russian government of having poisoned him on October 1st and unwisely a Russian Government statement hit back averring a CIA involvement:

> Probably, it is not the patient [Navalny] who works for the Western special services, but that the Western intelligence services who work with him – this would be more correct [to say]," *Dmitry Peskov explained.* "I can even be specific: these days, specialists from the Central Intelligence Agency of the United States of America are working with him.

But surely, that cannot be shown? It rather resembles a British Intel operation! Navalny replied on that same day:

> This is a direct allegation from a government official. Therefore, first of all, I am taking legal action against Peskov. And secondly, I demand that the proof and facts that suggest I am 'working with specialists from the CIA' are published. Put it straight on television, in prime time. You have my permission.

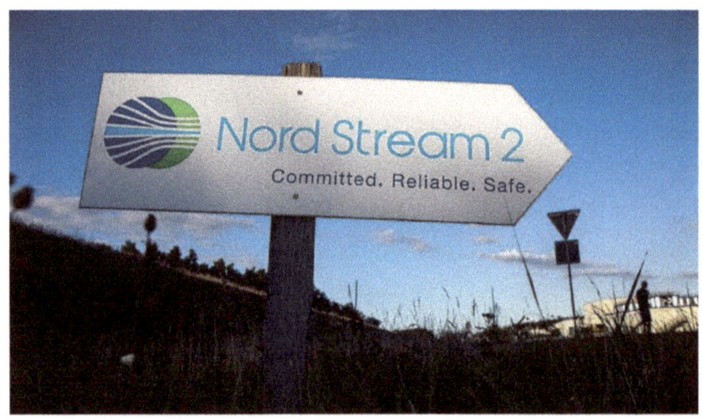

The near-completion of the NordStream II pipeline was the most compelling reason as to why Russia would *not* have ordered such an operation. Furthermore the recovering Mr Navalny could ask himself, why was he flown to Germany? He is after all not German. He was flown there on a pre-prepared plane[180] because this entire operation was designed to change the mind of Germany – and cancel the twenty billion Euros Nord Stream II project.

The OPCW Verdict

Any dose of Novichok which is survivable would not leave enough residue in blood or urine to be detectable. There is the *chemical* crux of the matter, due to its very high toxicity: intact Novichok cannot be detected in a victim who has survived! And that is especially so if days have already gone by after it was allegedly administered. That's a consequence of its great lethality.[181]

At Germany's request, on September 10th OPCW sent experts to collect biomedical samples from Navalny's blood and urine. This was three weeks after Navalny became ill and by this time he was well on the way to recovery. What could they hope to detect at this stage?

We can appreciate why the verdict from the Organization for the Prohibition of Chemical Weapons was greatly delayed, not emerging until the 6th of October. It was very vague about what had been found in his blood:

> The results of the analysis by the OPCW designated laboratories of biomedical samples collected by the OPCW team and shared with

180 'The flight was organized by an NGO whose backers and board members include Bill and Hillary Clinton, as well as the former German Chancellor Gerhard Schröder and his foreign minister, Joschka Fischer' (World Socialist Website 22 Sept., Clara Weiss).
Clearly, such an important flight was pre-arranged, as averred by Sergei Lavrov: "..the plane which was used to take him from Omsk… was ordered the day before he became unwell." (RT 28.1.22, 'Russia's Lavrov comments on Skripal Story'). For details on the pre-arranged flight see helmer.net, 'How the Navalny Novichok Operation was prepared – New Evidence from Germany,' 7.9.21.

181 www.fagain.co.uk/node/66 (rather arcane but clearly knows his subject)

> the Federal Republic of Germany confirm that the biomarkers of the cholinesterase inhibitor found in Mr Navalny's blood and urine samples have similar structural characteristics as the toxic chemicals belonging to schedules 1.A.14 and 1.A.15 that were added to the Annex on Chemicals to the Convention during the Twenty-Fourth Session of the Conference of the States Parties in November 2019. This cholinesterase inhibitor is not listed in the Annex on Chemicals to the Convention.[182]

The important statement here is that what they have detected was 'not listed' in their list of recognized poisons, which presumably means that it wasn't Novichok. One judgment here was:

> the analysed compound is apparently not officially prohibited under the Chemical Weapons Convention. As in the case of Skripal, when it is alleged to have been Novichok A234 , the OPCW does not use this term, nor does it speak directly of a chemical weapon, but rather indeterminately of a toxic chemical.[183]

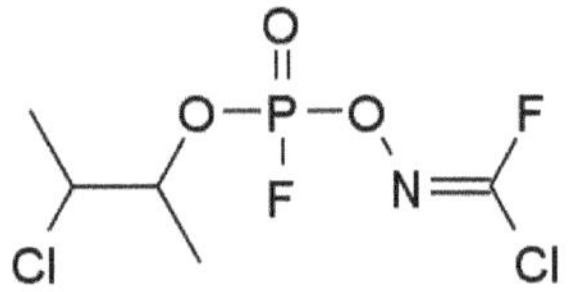

O
O–P–O F
F N=
Cl Cl

The OPCW merely claims to have found "biomarkers" of Navalny's metabolic disorder which may have been caused by some unidentified chemical poison. A chemist commented upon this:

> How really "similar" was it to Novichok nerve agent? For example, dichlorvos is also a cholinesterase inhibitor and "structurally similar" to many substances. The list of such substances is very wide.

There were therefore, he concluded, two likely options:

* Drug addict Navalny got an overdose of something that he has become used to eat, drink, sniff etc.

182https://www.opcw.org/media-centre/news/2020/10/opcw-issues-report-technical-assistance-requested-germany

183 Florian Roetzer in Telepolis (a German source): johnhelmer.net/urine-blood-hearsay-opcw-report-gives-the-german-game-away-reveals-no-novichok-weapon-no-navalny-crime/

* Maria Pevchikh, who spent the night in Navalny's room before the incident, poisoned him.[184]

If the latter, it's a British honey-trap! We look forward to developments in this story...

Blue Underpants

The water bottle story lasted from 17th September until 12th December, after which it faded away just like the earlier cup of tea story. The water bottle claim fell apart after it was pointed out that liquids cannot be taken through airport security, also CCTV footage showed Pevchikh buying water in the departure lounge. And so it was that on Saturday, December 12 *The Times* came out with its underpants story – someone had put Novichok onto his underpants! If so, how did they know which pair to smear it on? Apart from Marina Pevchikh, it was hard to imagine who could thus have had access to his underpants.

The Times two-page spread 'Kremlin made 2nd Attempt at Botched Assassination' claimed that the deadly poison was put onto Navalny's *underpants*. There would then have been three hours between his getting dressed that morning and collapsing on the plane.

The invisible poisoner would not have sneaked into the hotel room while Navalny was in the lounge bar that evening because he would then have been wearing his underpants. Did the unseen FSB agent tiptoe in later while Navalny was fast asleep? It would be a help if we had a public statement from the Xander Hotel itself.

The Times article – citing the usual anonymous 'sources' - reckoned that he had been poisoned *twice*, once in the hotel and a second time in the Siberian hospital at Omsk. People wondered how, if he had been poisoned twice with so deadly a substance, he made a complete recovery only weeks later? The hospital emergency crew at Omsk – who had probably saved his life – were understandably offended by this story,

184 southfront.org/navalnys-novichok-poisoning-fairy-tales-collapse-under-pressure-of-evidence/

with the chief toxicologist of the Omsk Region Alexander Sabaev stating categorically: "No one except medical professionals had access to his ward. This is all fiction – from beginning to end. There was no poisoning, either initial or secondary. This is fake news." (RT 14th December)

A mere two days after *The Times'* report a different version appeared this time from Bellingcat, the UK-government funded 'intelligence' unit.[185] These were the people (to remind the reader) who had claimed that the two Russians visiting Salisbury during the Skripal event (Petrov and Boshirov) were agents of the GRU, Russia's military intelligence agency, a claim they were never able to substantiate. By this version, late at night on August 19th in the bar of the Xander hotel, Navalny and his team were relaxing with some drinks. He ordered a cocktail and a barman served him with a 'Negroni.' After taking one sip of it he found that it tasted 'disgusting' – or, so he told Bellingcat.

Did that cause him to collapse from Novichok poisoning ten hours later? If so, it sounds even less credible than the Skripal poisoning story of two years earlier. Did the Xander Hotel have a waiter who put Novichok into a drink? If not, they should sue Bellingcat for this allegation!

On the same day as this Bellingcat report, the *New York Times* published a commentary on it, and added:

> Shortly after Mr. Navalny's arrival in Berlin, representatives from the Central Intelligence Agency and Britain's Secret Intelligence Service provided members of the German government with details about the poisoning, including the identities of the Federal Security Service officers involved, that directly implicated the Russian government, according to the senior German security official with knowledge of the matter.

So on the 22nd of August, as the unconscious Navalny was brought into the Berlin hospital, both CIA and MI6 were present and already had the story! That endorses the view here advocated.

The Bellingcat report featured a pack of FSB agents who had been following Navalny, and this part of the story was confirmed by Putin,

---

185 Bellingcat: 'FSB Team of Chemical Weapon Experts Implicated in Alexey Navalny Novichok Poisoning.' (14.12.20:) For an exposée see grayzone.com, 'Navalny poisoning: CIA, MI6, 'discredited' state-funded Bellingcat play key role in accusing Russia.' 27.12.20

though he denied they had tried to poison anyone. Navalny was being investigated for certain criminal charges which meant that he was forbidden to leave Russia and the only way he could get out was via the crisis that ensued, flying on a specially commissioned jet plane to Berlin.

On that same day the 14th of December, Navalny put though a telephone call to a FSB agent (Russian secret police) claiming to be a senior officer and demanding to know how the 'operation' had gone wrong. And this is three months later? We are told that this agent totally believed this impersonation without any verification and confessed to a stranger about the secret murder plan! He even offered the stranger (aka Navalny) a secure telephone number. He revealed that Novichok had been put onto (drum roll…) Navalny's blue underpants.

After he had been poisoned, the FSB agents managed to re-obtain said underpants some hours later - presumably this is in the Omsk hospital – and scrub off all trace of the deadly nerve agent! Then they cleverly dried them and put them back wherever they had been laid.[186] As to how the agents managed to gain entrance to the Omsk Clinical Emergency Hospital No. 1 and grab the underpants – wearing protective gloves no doubt – that may remind us of how the same agent had earlier gained access to Room No. 239 in the Xander Hotel in Tomsk, Siberia, and selected the underpants which Navalny would choose to wear the next day. Is it possible that any human being can believe such a tall story? Quite a lot of people could, it turned out.

And so the ever-changing story of how Alexei Navalny was 'poisoned' climaxed in December, *four months* after the event. The story was released on the winter solstice December 21st with a video by Navalny that gained ten million hits in one day. Demonstrations were soon taking place outside FSB offices in Russia, featuring blue underpants! Russian media publicized the shocking tale which was demoralizing for the Putin government.

The blue underpants, like the earlier bottle of water, soon disappeared. Navalny's wife Yulia Navalnaya claimed to have brought all of his clothes to the Berlin hospital, so surely the Berlin laboratory would at once have checked for presence of the deadly nerve agent? Can they not tell us the result of such testing?

---

186 *Moscow Times* 22.12.20 'Navalny's mock FSB Call'

Seven journalists writing in *Die Zeit* in September told how "the result of the analysis of the traces by the Institute of Pharmacology and Toxicology of the Bundeswehr' showed that 'scientists found corresponding residues on Navalny's hands and on the neck of a water bottle [Wasserflasche] from which he had been drinking.' Here was conclusive proof! We earlier quoted Merkel's spokesman as to how analysis of the water bottle brought from Siberia had shown 'definite proof' of fiendish intent. Where does that 'proof' stand now that the water bottle story has faded away and been replaced by blue underpants? Germans need to hold a symposium on this matter with open and frank discussion, to try and ascertain who was lying to who. Do they have *any* reliable measurements? How come top levels of the German government endorsed the water bottle story? Is it really worth cancelling a pipeline for such a tale?

Had a deadly nerve poison been absorbed around the crotch in a lethal quantity, would not excruciating pain have been experienced in a most sensitive region of a man's anatomy? Would Navalny even have got as far as the airport? His thighs would have marks of inflammation showing the near-lethal event, which the medics at Omsk would have noted: but clearly nothing like that did happen because all of the earlier stories - three of them – featured poison ingested from a drink. At no point in his graphic accounts of what he had suffered was any pain or irritation of his crotch area suggested nor did the doctors at Omsk notice any such thing.

This new video had Navalny claiming 'I spoke to my assassin,' viz. that he had put through a call to one of the FSB agents trying to poison him. The day after, the Former State Duma Deputy Gennady Gudkov wrote on Facebook that Navalny's investigations mean Russia "has entered a new phase in the recognition of the criminal character and complete amorality of the Putin regime.... Russia is ruled by a criminal band that has seized power and in order to continue its usurpation is prepared to undertake openly monstrous crimes." In a similar vein of damnation the lawyer Vasily Shlykov thundered: "According to the codes of the Russian-speaking world, any officer and soldier who has sworn an oath to the Fatherland must, after such a thing, shoot himself.

Putin is an officer! Russia has never seen such a shameful thing!!"[187] Strong language indeed and deep passions are being aroused here. A Navalny-versus-Putin confrontation has been set up. Public and open discussion of the issues involved *needs to happen,* being the only way forward capable of rescuing the situation.

To try and get a focus upon what *did* happen, it may help to listen to a former senior US Intel agent on the topic:

> The poisoning happened on 20 August, the 'hoax call' is made on 14 December, and released by Bellingcat on 21 December. Now, wait a minute. The context of the call, a desperate demand for answers of what went wrong (Navalny didn't die) for a report to higher-up authority, is something you would expect within the first 48 hours, not nearly three months later.
>
> Bellingcat is an organization created around the idea of 'the Russians did it' (or the Russians should be held responsible, even if they didn't do it) world information warfare stage from Syria chemical warfare crimes to MH17 to the Skripal poisoning to (now) Navalny (and whatever else escapes my memory at the moment.)
>
> He's too slow & dumb (the FSB guy) he should have been wide awake by now, this all seems scripted. Do we know it is actually the Russian officer on the other end? Rather, is it a MI6 or CIA actor? In the very early stages (long before the 14th minute), the 'Russian' intelligence officer should have demanded to make the call himself, calling back from a secure phone to his interrogator (after confirming with his own chain of command), at the least. I can't believe the Russians are without strict protocol training in this regard.
>
> This raises a related issue; why would someone who'd so famously screwed up a hit still be on the job?
>
> Then, at 18 minutes in, the Russian troglodyte is volunteering an investigative supervisor's phone number to a 'superior officer' (Navalny's alias) he has never even heard of.
>
> The concluding question should be, did Nalvany understand he

187 Radio Free Europe, 22.12.20 'Russian Watergate': Russian Social Media Reacts After Navalny 'Dupes' FSB Agent On His Poisoning.'

> had been talking to a Western intelligence asset/actor? The answer would be "probably not." Narcissists are brilliant material for intelligence agency manipulations, in this case Nalvany being of far greater value as an information operations asset in Berlin as opposed to a perpetually failed color revolutionary in Russia.[188]

If Navalny really believed his own story, then assuredly he ought to initiate a lawsuit of conspiracy to commit murder against the FSB agent Konstantin Kudryavtsev, to whom he allegedly spoke on the phone. Then we'd at least be able to see that agent and hear his view – which no-one has to-date. Things need to be brought out into the open and not covered over in silence and a court case would do that. All the world would listen!

In the Blood

As with the Skripal event, we end up with no-one being too sure of what happened, that being the nature of an intelligence operation.

The Omsk doctors at the Emergency Hospital found indicators of a severe metabolic disorder from their blood and urine measurements which might well account for his sudden blackout. Was it too much alcohol the night before acting in synergy with the various pills he was taking, maybe anti-depressants, too much sex with Marina Pevchikh and not enough sleep? But, let us listen to the diagnosis.

Navalny's blood and urine contained propofol, pentibarbitone, diazepam and caffeine, whereas the by-products of Novichok poisoning called 'cholinesterase inhibitors' were absent. Dr Alexander Sabaev, the chief toxicologist who was the first to treat Navalny, said the patient was put on a ventilator and into an induced coma and given the emergency drug atropine. 'His blood levels were found to be 'six times higher than the norm for amylase, sugar and serum lactate; twice the normal level of leukocytosis and the maximum level of acetonuria. In addition, alcohol, (0.2 ppm) was found in the urine... these are the metabolites, the

188 'the Hoax Call' Ronald Thomas West 23.12.2020

substances which have been produced. These substances in large quantities cause pathological changes.' If Navalny did not suffer from diabetes, the tests showed that he had an acute metabolic disorder. 'An increase in the level of acetate and lactic acid, its excessive formation makes acidification of the blood. It should not be in such a quantity. There should be an indicator, let's say two; but we had an indicator of twelve, that is six times more.' The level of internal acetone in Navalny's body was at a maximum: 'normally acetone should be negative that is it should be excreted from the body ... in this case the carbohydrate metabolism suffered and completely different scenarios of development occurred. The body began to destroy itself from the inside.'[189]

We're not too sure what he meant by that least remark but let's remember that Navalny had just been though quite a stressful and exhausting campaign (concerning elections in Tomsk) and a relapse in the aftermath of such a program of activities is by no means uncommon.

A consensus seems to be emerging that a combination of alcohol, lithium and benzos taken by Navalny himself were involved and that he had suffered a grand seizure due to hyperglycemia after going into diabetic shock. The doctors at Omsk were emphatic that they had found no trace of toxic substances in his liver, kidneys of lungs, which led them to conclude that whatever happened was caused by a metabolic disorder. The lithium as found in his blood is commonly used to treat bipolar disorders. From a combination of these drugs Navalny would have suffered dramatic cholinesterase inhibition effects before his collapse on the plane.

One may regret that the unconscious Navalny could not have stayed one more day in that Omsk hospital, after which he might have recovered more and a clearer diagnosis been achieved. The 'blame' here such as it is falls upon Vladimir Putin. Navalny's wife contacted him and begged for her husband to be allowed to travel to Germany: so Putin contacted the Prosecutor General's Office, to allow him to go abroad – owing to criminal charges pending against him this had been prohibited. That ban was waived enabling him to travel abroad. In a rational world such

189 Report by Alexander Sabaev, Omsk Hospital 12.10.20, trans. from Russian by John Helmer: 'German Defence Ministry ordered the Swedish defence laboratory to find Novichok in Navalny's blood.'

events would absolve the Russians of guilt.

Hunting Wild Boar

Navalny was released from the Charité medical clinic on September 22nd

a week after he woke up, but he did not return to Russia for another *four months*, not until January 17th. During that time he enjoyed jogging over the German countryside, taking long walks through the woods and chasing wild boar!

<u>Figure:</u> Alexei Navalny goes jogging in Germany

The forests he visited included the Black Forest of southwestern Germany and the Swiss woods around Basel, Switzerland. On the ground in the Black Forest he was surrounded by more than one hundred police and secret service agents; in the air above, there were helicopter patrols and electronic signal monitoring aircraft. Roadblocks, checkpoints, and even an encrypted communication tower, specially set up for him the day before his arrival, caused more dismay and discussion among the villagers. The German security services set up a special communications tower in Ibach village.

"So the whole region where the Kremlin critic was staying was under police protection. In the streets and around the cottage the officials patrolled. I've never seen anything like it," remarked the Swiss Franz Stadelmann who became a friend of Navalny and joined his *entourage*: "Even as we walked into the woods with Navalny, police ran in front of and behind us." He introduced them to boar hunting, or tried to. One participant remarked, "We haven't seen a single boar. But that was logical with all the policemen running around in the woods for Navalny's protection. They scared the animals away."

Figure: A healthy fellow, post-Novichok??

The whole 'Operation Waldeinsamkeit' as it was called, cost the German state more than €25 million in men and equipment[190] and one would appreciate further discussion as to why they did this and when it was planned. A US company rented the Black Forest Studios so that Navalny's video could be produced there from December 30 to January 13. He there made the video under the protection of German security experts. The identity of the US contractor who paid the costs of the entire production, remains secret.

190 Estimate by John Helmer (ref. 107 above) based on 'what German sources in the area, and also in Berlin' had told him (personal comm.).

Figure: with his *entourage* in the Black Forest

It seems likely that Navalny was in Basel shortly after he was released from the Charité Hospital in Berlin. He would have been in Switzerland between September 25 and 30. It is not clear what he was doing there and what role the Swiss government played in guarding him, but his visit went unreported in the Swiss media.[191] From October 1, he started giving a series of interviews in Berlin, and the German and international media then published photographs of him in the city. On October 14 the German security forces flew him to the little village of Ibach in the Black Forest. There was a gym there, and 'Whenever Navalny was at a training session, the gym was closed by the police to everyone else.' This was a high-security operation.

'Putin's Palace'

After his recovery Navalny and his team spent two weeks in the rented German film studio together with a los Angeles production crew, and created the two-hour long anti-Putin video. It accused him of secretly building a glorious palace for his private residence, at a cost of $1.3 billion. Strategically released two days after Navalny's re-entry into Russia on January 17th, it had soon – apparently - logged up one hundred million views.[192] He called for nationwide anti-Putin protests to take place on January 23rd.

The film described a palace of immense opulence complete with gambling salon, aqua-disco and a saucy pole-dance room with deep red

191 http://johnhelmer.net/alexei-navalnys-waldeinsamkeit-thats-german-for-spiritual-forest-walking-surrounded-by-100-german-secret-service-agents/#more-45946

192 But NB these may have been fabricated. About 17% of Russians watched it, half for less than two minutes: Helmer 9.2.21

wallpaper, but it turned out alas that none of that actually existed. Putin denied that he owned it, saying that neither he nor any relatives of his had been there and that pictures of him swimming there had been photoshopped. Journalists visiting the place were startled to find an unfinished concrete building nowhere near to being inhabitable. Locals living on the remote peninsula – which does not even have a railway line – were startled by the electrifying publicity. A Russian billionaire stepped forward and declared that he owned it, saying it would be ready as a luxury hotel in a few years! Commented RT News:

> In late January, reporters from the *Mash* news channel visited the property. However, instead of being met by butlers and offered a flutter in the private casino, they found only an unfinished shell and a group of slightly bemused construction workers. The channel's editor-in-chief, Maxim Iksanov, described it as *"a big pile of concrete"*... Surrounded by scaffolding, the building has been only partly completed from the outside, while the interior is effectively a shell, with wires hanging from un-plastered walls. Across 16 identical rooms, bags of concrete are stacked up, with the swimming pool and much of the garden still unfinished.'[193]

Figure: Russian billionaire Arkady Romanovich, owner of the jGelendzhik hotel construction

Here is *concrete* proof, of mendacity on the part of Alexei Navalny, allegedly the great truth-teller.

193 RT 29 Jan 'Building dubbed Putin's Palace is an Empty Shell'; 8 Feb., 'One in 4 saw Navalny's Putin's Palace documentary.'

For a judgement here let's turn to John Helmer. He first quotes a Russian commentator on the Palace:

> Now Navalny says this again, but does not mention that there is no evidence of Putin's presence there. Because the impudence of his lying has increased many times in ten years...But there is no smoke without fire. What is the reality? this palace [comes from] a group of rich people who are also personally well acquainted with Putin, and [who] decided around 2005 to build a house for him when he resigns from the post of president. But Putin refused to accept such a gift from them.

It seems to have been built originally by a consortium of businessmen who had thought they could somehow offer it to Putin, but that did not work out.

Figure: The sultry Hookah Room set up for pole-dancing in Putin's $1.3 billion secret palace – according to Mr Navalny

Navalny's speech during the video appeared as if reading a US script, for example it alluded to the 'mud room' of the Palace which has no translation in Russian, whereas it is a commonly used term in American real estate parlance to signify a semi-outdoor room next to a garden:

> Linguistic analysis of Navalny's video on the Gelendzhik palace indicates the English subtitles were written first, and then translated for Navalny to speak in Russian. The English is

> American, not British; and certainly not the English of the German and American operatives who provided the video production technology, editing, and special effects at the Black Forest Studios in Kirchzarten, Germany. According to a German press report from Kirchzarten, "the studio bosses remember that at the beginning of December, a request by email came from a production company in Los Angeles. There was talk of a documentary...In terms of content, the Black Forest Studios have nothing to do with the film, the studio owners emphasize. They only provided the technology and the location and organized the shooting.

Helmer concludes:

> How is it possible for a 44-year old native Russian-speaker with two Moscow university degrees and years of experience in Russian public speaking to make such clumsy mistakes? How is it possible for this figure to fabricate the stories of his poisonings so often that he can't remember the last fabrication he told, or the contradictions between them he expects his audience to ignore? The answer is that he is a presenter with a script composed by others.[194]

Some years earlier, the Anti-Corruption Foundation had been caught soliciting funds from MI6, as a recently-released Russian Intel video[195] showed. The FBK's executive director was cleverly caught asking: 'If we had more money, we would expand our team, of course,' adding that his goal of obtaining 'a little money,' like '10, 20 million dollars a year would make a huge difference.' Definitely. He described his organization's activities as 'mass protests, civil initiatives, propaganda, establishing contacts with the elite and explain to them that we are reasonable people and we are not going to demolish everything and take away their assets.' He named some top Russian businessmen and asked if MI6 could give some lowdown on them!

How is it possible that these people have not been charged with treason? The video greatly implicates the British Government in Navalny's cause. His FBK party has been assigned the status of a foreign agent and not a Russian opposition party. It has been widely accused of

---

194 Dances with Bears, 'Oligarchy in Russia – Alexei Navalny's telling Mistake' 25.1.21

195 See RT, 'Explosive video exposes MI6 links to Alexei Navalny' (1.2.21) as a coup by Russian counter-intelligence plus pungent comments by Rick Sanchez.

treasonous behavior, especially after it sent a letter to the new President Joe Biden calling for US sanctions against a number of prominent Russian politicians.

Convicted for Fraud

Charges filed against the Navalny brothers were for embezzlement amounting to more than 26 million rubles (nearly $850,000) and both were convicted of fraud and money-laundering. In 2008 while holding an important tax position with the Russian postal service, Alexei and his younger brother Oleg manipulated the cosmetic giant Yves Rocher to sign a contract for cargo mail with a shell company *Glavnoye Podpisnoye Agentstvo* (or Main Subscription Agency) based in Cyprus which he had secretly created without the firm's knowledge.[196] Cyprus is a notorious money-laundering haven. The company provided shipping services to Yves Rocher's Vostok branch at an inflated cost.

Then in 2012 as an advisor to the governor of the Kirov province Nikita Belykh Navalny arranged fraudulent contracts with a timber firm, using his position to circumvent the law. He was charged with stealing about $500,000 worth of illegally harvested timber. According to the prosecution, Navalny partnered with Director Petr Ofitserov of Vyatka Forest Products Company and Vyacheslav Opalev, Director of the local bank, in order to illegally harvest 10,000 cubic meters (over 13,000 cubic yards) of timber valued at more than 16 million rubles ($500,000) on state forest land.

In 2014 he was charged and convicted of fraud and embezzlement involving these two firms, 'Yves Rocher' and the Russian state-owned timber firm, altogether totalling about $1,000,000. He was placed under house arrest while he was being investigated on suspicion of embezzlement, then in December the two brothers were convicted by a Russian court on charges of embezzling 30 million rubles (= $442,000) from the Russian branch of Yves Rocher and another firm.

For the first offence he received a 3 ½ year sentence and for the second,

196 katehon.com/en/article/cognitive-breakdown-navalny-hoax-american-imperialism-and-media-censorship 24.2.21

a 5-year sentence but both were suspended, whereas his brother was jailed.

Having his brother put in jail for a case he considered to be unjust, would strongly tend to polarise his views: especially after 2017 when the European Court of Human rights ruled that the case against the two Navalnys had been 'arbitrary and manifestly unreasonable,'[197] endorsing Navalny's claim that the prosecutions were politically-motivated. It was "apparent that he had been treated in that way in order to curtail his public activities" it averred - and mandated Russia to pay him compensation! The ECHR again ruled in Navalny's favour in 2019. Further discussion of this matter could be helpful, as on the face of it such claims would appear to be unsound.[198]

Jail: Birth of a Hero?

Chronology

<u>January 2021</u>

17 Navalny returns to Russia, is arrested.

20 He lodges complaint to the ECHR

21 Release of his video on Putin

22 A letter by Mr Kozak doubts his 'poisoning.'

23 Street demonstrations pro-Navalny

27 Putin's Davos speech

29 FSB sends letter to Joe Biden, urging sanctions.

31 Russians join street demonstrations.

<u>February</u>

2 Navalny is tried & sentenced

5 EU representative Borrel visits Lavrov in Moscow

9 Borrell speech to EU parliament on failure of hismission

14 Nationwide Valentine's Day evening flashlight demos

197 For Navalny's point of view see www.navalny.com

198 For insightful comments here, see Matthew Johnson *Op. cit.* katehon.com 'cognitive breakdown Navalny hoax'.

16 2nd trial for defamation case

16 Panel of ECHR judges demand his 'immediate' release.

In December 2014, Navalny had been given a suspended sentence of three and a half years of imprisonment on fraud charges, which probationary period had been extended until December 2020. He repeatedly violated its terms, leading to his arrest on January 17. The Federal Penitentiary Service had warned him before his arrival in Moscow that violations of the requirements of the suspended sentence would oblige them to go to court with a request to replace the suspended sentence with a real one. Navalny and his allies in the West knew what he was facing, but decided to go ahead.

'I would like to remind you that Navalny is the only twice conditionally convicted person in Russia. Such extraordinary leniency of the court was never applied to anyone else,' prosecutor Ekaterina Fokina told TASS: as if the authorities were nervous of the international ethical damnation that would follow.

For the demonstrations that followed on 23rd of January, the optics were terrible: black-clad Russian police with batons attacking the young pro-Navalny demonstrators, with thousands turning out in nearly two hundred towns and cities. After a repeat demonstration a week later, three diplomats one of them German were expelled for allegedly having participated in these unauthorised demonstrations, or being present at them. Some five thousand people were arrested in the two weekends of demonstrations.

At his court case on February 2nd Navalny gave an unhinged speech saying that he did not recognize the court trying him, it was 'completely illegal…' and claiming that Russia's President would be called 'Vladimir the Underpants Poisoner.' The stressed-out nonagenarian who had brought the case had to leave and was taken home in an ambulance. It all sounds rather Dostoievskian.

As Alexei Martynov, a well-known political commentator in Russia, observed: 'It seemed to Navalny that he does not live like everyone else, but participates in some kind of virtual game, that he is the hero of an adventure film. And then he suddenly found himself in a real court, behind bars. Of course, an unpleasant sobering up.' The sentence was two years and eight months.

The UK's Foreign Minister Dominic Raab read out a statement condemning the verdict as "Today's perverse ruling, targeting the victim of a poisoning rather than those responsible…' Let's note that all of the discussion, all of the polemic, all of the ethical damnation, hinges upon the presumption that somebody had attempted to poison him, which is never examined or debated but merely presumed. That is the world we live in.

The 'High Representative of the European Union' Josep Borrell came to visit Sergei Lavrov on 5th February in a last attempt to patch up good relations, but notice of the three European diplomats being expelled was released during his visit and scuppered the endeavour. The US *Radio Liberty* released the news. Upon returning home Borrell encountered widespread dissatisfaction with his visit and 81 MEPs signed a petition demanding his resignation on the grounds that he had not 'stood up' to Russia properly.

Borrell's report to the EU parliament expressed a growing mistrust between the European Union and Russia, a view that relations had 'hit rock bottom.' The purpose of his visit had been, he said -

> First, to convey, eye to eye, face to face, the European Union's position on matters of concern to us: human rights, political freedoms and the situation of Mr [Alexei] Navalny. This I did and they [the Russian authorities] did not appreciate [it]: the case of Alexei Navalny was at the centre of my tense exchange with Minister [for Foreign Affairs or Russia, Sergei] Lavrov.'[199]

He called for Mr Navalny's 'immediate and unconditional release', which was rather impertinent, as well as for 'a full and impartial investigation into his assassination attempt.' Given the absolute refusal of the German government to share an iota of their laboratory data concerning Navalny's blood and urine – as they are obliged to do under the OPCW regulations – that request seems rather disingenuous. Russia has explained that it would be happy to open a criminal investigation if that data were shared, because only then might they have evidence of a crime committed, viz. poisoning. As Mr Lavrov kept trying to explain to

199 Eeas.europa.eu Russia: Speech by High Representative/Vice-President Josep Borrell at the EP debate on his visit to Moscow 9.2.21

Borrell, the only medical expertise to which they have access, i.e. those at the Omsk hospital, had failed to detect any evidence of poisoning.

One gained the impression that the entire meaning of Borrell's visit to Moscow along with East-West relations revolved around Mr Navalny's fate, as if he had not deserved his (fairly short) prison sentence.

Navalny found himself facing a second trial a week after that earlier one, for defamatory comments which he had addressed to a 95 year old Russian war veteran, hero of the Great Patriotic War. He had appeared in a state video a year ago, in which several persons spoke out on RT concerning a vote to adjust the Russian constitution. Navalny – who reckoned the adjustments gave Putin undue powers - called those who appeared in it 'traitors', 'corrupt lackeys', a 'disgrace to the country' and 'people without a conscience.' The distressed nonagenarian not surprisingly pressed defamation charges. At the trial Navalny raved on about how the old man was mentally unable to follow the proceedings and called the judge 'the must unscrupulous judge in the world.'

The 95-year old veteran was hoping merely to receive some sort of apology in the court, which would have satisfied him. Instead, Navalny repeatedly called him a 'doll' who 'does not understand anything' and who is 'traded' by his family adding that 'his relatives will strangle him tonight.' The veteran's grandson asked the blogger to 'remain a man' during the testimony. Navalny's response included shouting that 'the only problem with your grandfather is that he raised a grandson who is a prostitute.'

RIA Novosti, a state news agency, published a report on the trial by Irina Alksnis, entitled, *Navalny destroyed himself as a politician in one day*:

> Against this background, Navalny's constant shift into shouting, rolling into hysterics, bickering with the court, and insulting other participants in the process look like trifles. Although at some point, the judge, unable to stand the circus, gave five minutes to the lawyers to 'bring the defendant to his senses', since 'there is no longer any possibility to tolerate this...The main result of today was the public elimination of Alexei Navalny himself as a socio-political figure.

Some will continue to support Mr Navalny she reckoned, 'But by doing so, they will spread to themselves something monstrous in its immorality and inhumanity, which looked out today from under the usual cosmetically perfect mask of the opposition – and from which everyone else recoiled in horror.'[200]

He was fined the equivalent of £9,300. Considering that Navalny and his team have received around $300,000 in bitcoin donations during the month of January, and that overall his two wallets have received 730 bitcoin since their creation, which is now worth in the region of a staggering $35 million, the fine handed down to him on Feb 16th is insignificant. It does not harm him at all. That is a remarkably timid sentence for his having scoffed at a court and reiterated the defamatory language with which he had been charged. In the UK such behaviour would certainly have earned extra jail time.

Images of pro-Navalny demos across Russia (www.navalny.com), as people emerged with flashlights on the evening of Valentine's day

At a final hearing to confirm the sentence, Navalny told the judge that she should go home and make some pickle, and finally told members of the court that they would all 'burn in hell.'

Navalny's aides organised a couple of street demos followed by a romantic Valentine's Day flashlight event. Pictures show the latter, where he reckoned on his website that:

- more than 10,000 photos and videos of the action were sent to our telegram bot from all over Russia;

200 Johnhelmer.net 'Alexei Navalny crashes out' 9.2.21

- more than 11,000 posts about the campaign on Instagram, excluding stories;
- more than 37,000 posts on Twitter with the hashtag #LoveStrongerFear.

Is this the emergence of a new grass-roots political movement in Russia? It could be, and in the meantime we can't help noticing that his jail conditions must be remarkably lax, if he was able to co-organize a nationwide demo and then post up a moving account of it on his personal website. This was complete with his usual sneering comments against the government of his country and its President.

Since he was put in jail, he has been receiving awesome accolades from Euro-groups. Thus –

On February 17th the **Council of Europe** stated:

> We deeply regret the recent decision of a Moscow court to sentence Alexei Navalny to a prison term. This decision is based on a criminal conviction which the European Court of Human Rights, in its *Navalnyye v. Russia* judgment of 17 October 2017, found to have been arbitrary and manifestly unreasonable and, as a consequence, in violation of Articles 6 and 7 of the European Convention on Human Rights, to which Russia is a party. We call upon the Russian authorities to abide by their international obligations.

On February 23rd the **Geneva Summit for Human Rights and Democracy** (a part of the UN Human rights Council) awarded him their

'Courage Prize', for 'inspiring the world with his extraordinary courage in the defence of Justice and Human rights.'

(on that same day, Amnesty International announced that it was stripping Navalny of his prisoner of conscience status, because he 'advocated violence and discrimination'. They had been receiving a flood of complaints alleging that various racist and 'far-right' political statements of his constituted 'hate speech.')

On March 1st **The United Nations** at Geneva: two UN human rights experts called for an international investigation into the 'poisoning' of Navalny, and released the text of a long letter they had earlier sent to the Russian authorities.

On March 11th the **Committee of Ministers of the Council of Europe** (a body which oversees ECHR decisions) demanded that Navalny be released immediately on the grounds that he was innocent. The Navalny brothers had only been doing that which was 'indistinguishable from normal commercial activities.' They had been sentenced 'on the basis of judicial decisions that were arbitrary, unforeseen and manifestly unfounded,' it claimed.

As to whether it is the business of the ECHR to interfere with domestic lawcourt decisions: the ECHR protocols state that 'The Court does not question the interpretation and application of national law by national courts unless there has been a flagrant non-observance or arbitrariness in the application of that law.' It seems clear that neither of those conditions apply here.

A huge pro-Navalny demo was planned all across Russia for the spring, aiming to have half a million turnout, but in the end somewhat over ten thousand turned out. Here is the view of a well-known political commentator Richard Lendemann:

> CIA asset, Western media darling, political nobody Navalny is imprisoned for 2.8 years near Moscow – for multiple breaches of his suspended sentence. Along with embezzling millions of dollars for self-enrichment, he's guilty of sedition.
>
> Serving as an unregistered US foreign agent, he operated as a fifth column threat against his homeland...Navalny got off easily. Instead of long-term imprisonment for betraying his country and

grand theft, his sentence is short-term.[201]

On May 7th, **Amnesty International** re-designated Navalny as a 'Prisoner of Conscience,' on the absurd grounds that 'he has been imprisoned for demanding a government that is free from corruption.' In 2007 while campaigning as a white nationalist for the Russian National Liberation Movement (which he co-founded) he made a pro-gun rights video about wanting to exterminate 'flies and cockroaches' – alluding to Muslims. In the video he is seen pulling out a gun and shooting a Muslim. After the shocking violence of this act, he calmly states 'In such cases I recommend a handgun.' He has never repudiated such views, quite the contrary. Earlier in the year Amnesty had scruples about supporting a man with such unapologetically racist views, but has now got over these. In the UK a person expressing such views would simply not be able to speak in public and would surely be jailed for hate speech.

Détente Disintegrates

The Nord Stream pipelines are due to deliver one hundred billion cubic metres of natural gas yearly, from Russia to Germany. But will this happen? The Skripal and Navalny episodes together have exercised a profound impact in degrading and undermining East-West détente, and by 2021 it was evident that a new Cold War 2.0 was freezing over. The

201 21st Century Wire, Stephen Lendeman: 'Fake news about Navalny's politicised Imprisonment,' 20.4.21.

fate of the splendid new pipeline - seven hundred and sixty miles long, the longest in the world - hangs in the balance. Fictional horror has proved itself to be a reliable path to 'success', even towards EU unity, *because* no public media has the will to deconstruct this highly-developed 21st -century art form. The politicians are not *as such* total liars - rather it is Those Who Create Delusion i.e. military intelligence who fabricate stories through that Hall of Mirrors which is British intelligence. The politicians merely believe them, insofar as they believe anything.

In November of 2020, *fifty-six nations* at an OPCW conference had issued a joint statement condemning Russia, on the grounds that it had allegedly poisoned Mr Navalny using a banned chemical substance. The fact that he appeared to be quite well and strolling about – in fact, jogging over the hills - soon after the event was not a problem. They sent an instruction to Russia, that she should "disclose in a swift and transparent manner the circumstances of this chemical attack."[202] That is like posing the question: When did you stop beating your wife? Moreover the tone of that request is threatening as if addressing a naughty schoolboy. Russia has repeatedly requested both the OPCW and the German authorities for a sharing of data and results of analysis of the blood and urine of Mr Navalny – as is in fact mandated by OPCW protocols - and been refused. Had it been shared, Russia would have been in some degree able to answer the OPCW request.

Here is Sergei Lavrov, sadly ruminating (on Russian radio) upon the disintegration of détente, *caused by* the absence of honesty in the words of politicians:

> When the European Union is speaking as a superior, Russia wants to know, can we do any business with Europe? ... The people who are responsible for foreign policy in the West do not understand the necessity of mutual respect in dialogue. And then probably for some time we have to stop talking to them...
>
> No matter what we do, the West will try to hobble and restrain us, and undermine our efforts in the economy, politics, and technology. These are all elements of one approach.

202 'Joint statement from the 25th Session of Conference of State Parties to the OPCW on Monday, November 30.'

> Question: Their national security strategy states that they will do so.
>
> Lavrov: Of course it does, but it is articulated in a way that decent people can still allow to go unnoticed, but it is being implemented in a manner that is nothing short of outrageous.
>
> ... they clearly want to throw us off balance, and not only by direct attacks on Russia in all possible and conceivable spheres by way of unscrupulous competition, illegitimate sanctions and the like, but also by unbalancing the situation near our borders, thus preventing us from focusing on creative activities. Nevertheless, regardless of the human instincts and the temptations to respond in the same vein, I'm convinced that we must abide by international law.[203]

Here is a general comment made by the World Socialist Website:

> The Navalny case bears all the hallmarks of a major political provocation. On a factual level, nothing makes sense. While the imperialist powers unanimously proclaim that he has been poisoned with the nerve agent Novichok, one of the deadliest poisons in the world, Navalny has almost recovered within weeks with no apparent lasting damage, and is now hammering away at the Putin regime on social media.[204]

Compare that with a judgment from a conservative US group, the Larouche Foundation:

> The British chemical weapons lab at Porton Down has "confirmed" that Russian opposition figure Navalny was poisoned by Novichok—just as they "determined" that Russian double agent Sergei Skripal had been poisoned by Putin, and as the "White Helmets"—whose co-founder was a "former" MI6 operative—insisted that the Assad government was using chemical weapons against their own citizens! What each of these stories has in common is a featured role played by British intelligence, such as that played by "former" MI6 operative Christopher Steele, in fabricating the story of Russia's role in electing Donald Trump. Do

---

203 Pepe Escobar 20.10.20 unz.com/pescobar/russia-and-the-eu-business-as-usual-is-over/
204 Wsws.org 'EU Parliament calls for int. investigation…' 22.9.20

> they think we won't notice that these stories are always circulated to disrupt summits between Trump and Putin, or Trump and Xi, to sabotage the potential for the collaboration of great powers?[205]

'Gladio' in the last century was a NATO deep state operation to ensure that a proper fear of communism endured throughout Europe, by creating terror events of its own.[206] By means of this Black Art a phantom 'enemy' is conjured up. Rather surprisingly, its spirit does indeed survives to this day and is being resuscitated: all these events have that flavour. One could here congratulate the British cold warriors – the *7/7 Brigade* at Newbury, *Bellingcat, the Integrity Initiative, Institute for statecraft* - who have helped to pull off these spectacularly successful hoaxes.

Vlad: the world's most vilified, but also the second most popular, politician (China's President Xi usually comes first)

'The threat of the beginning of the struggle of all against all' was the theme of President Vladimir Putin's online address to the Davos Forum of January 27th 2021, his first since 2009. He warned about a possible global conflict similar to the Second World War:

> Humanity is at risk of losing entire civilizational and cultural continents. Our common responsibility today is to avoid such a prospect, which looks like a gloomy dystopia, and to ensure development along a different, positive, harmonious and

205 https://larouchepac.com/20200903/just-how-stupid-do-they-think-we-are Sept 3rd briefing

206 Richard Cottrell, *Gladio NATO's dagger at the Heart of Europe* 2015.

constructive trajectory.

Despite this looming threat, he reaffirmed his optimistic vision of Europe as a culture at peace with itself:

> If we can rise above these problems of the past and get rid of these phobias, then we will certainly enjoy a positive stage in our relations. We are ready for this, we want this, and we will strive to make this happen. But love is impossible if it is declared only by one side. It must be mutual.

A US commentator asked, 'Did you happen to catch the most important political speech of the past six years?' alluding to this Putin speech at Davos. He added, 'I don't get the sense from anything I've seen from the Biden Administration or the European Commission in Brussels that anyone *heard a word he said*.'[207] In truth, *no notice* was taken of this vitally important statement by the Western media, it being drowned out by the Navalny affair. His speech had made dismissive allusions to the 'Great Reset.' which probably accounted for the media blackout, the 'Great Reset' being the dominant theme of that year's Davos conference. Putin had objected to its robotic, soulless, globalist vision of the future where everyone has to be vaccinated.

On several occasions President Putin has given such warnings, and one can hardly avoid noticing that only the Russians seem troubled by this prospect. Which is easy to understand: the NATO nations of Europe make a habit of their *braggadocio* behavior, routinely insulting and threatening Russia, knowing that their expenditure on military is about two dozen times that of Russia, plus they are backed up by America. It appears that they thereby experience some sort of togetherness.

The combination of expelling diplomats while moving NATO military equipment ever closer to Russia's border is pure madness. We may assume it will lead to what it looks as if it were intended to lead to, viz. nuclear war in Eastern Europe within the next decade. Europeans may believe that US military hardware is there to 'defend Europe' (from what?) however from a US point of view the treaties can easily be flipped

---

207 Sott.net 'Great Reset? Putin says, Not so fast!' tom Luongo, 10.2.21

over into a warfighting scenario.[208] The US may have wargamed outcomes where it benefits from war in Europe, as removing their main economic competitor, making their president more popular, etc. War in Europe may be fairly congenial for the USA, for did it not benefit greatly from the two previous world wars? There may even be a sense in which nuclear war limited to Europe would be convenient for the two superpowers. The US withdrawal from the INF treaty in 2019 enables a host of 'intermediate range' nuclear weapons to be positioned around Russia by the USA. If Europe has felt fairly safe from the danger of nuclear war for several decades it was because of that now-expired treaty.

We have here examined the *tactics of deception*, in relation to how three cases of alleged poisonings were blamed on Russia and in fact upon President Putin personally - but which seem to have had their origin in British Deep State machinations. These events have been spectacularly successful in their goals of degrading East-West relations, extinguishing diplomacy, promoting military morale, making nuclear war in Europe more likely and generally creating a sense of horror. What I call the *Phantom Menace* is essential for maintaining the big military budgets to keep people living in fear. That illusory menace lives and breathes through the false-flag terror events (Appendix 3). Public airing and discussion of these fabricated events would be necessary, if we ever wished to enter a world that could be worth living in, where some degree of honesty and truth prevailed in international relations.

The people of Europe are not likely to get any new palaces of culture or temples of amusement or glorious new cities and instead the surplus revenue will be going to the military for their horrible new megadeath weapons. We are sinking into a new cold war *caused by* the mental laziness of people in believing the fear-porn and fabricated terror-threats, churned out by the media and politicians.

---

208 Novostipmr.com Alexey Martynov: 'USA involves Russia into an armed conflict in the center of Europe:' 'Europe has suddenly begun to understand what is done with it and what will be done with it very soon,' 11.8.17.

Epilogue ...and so to WW3

Europe had a prospective future ahead of peace and prosperity: all it had to do was to switch on the Nordstream-II pipeline and refrain from bringing NATO right up against the borders of Russia. Was that so hard?

Germany in particular was co-signator of the Minsk Agreement and this was the peace plan for the Ukraine: to be a neutral and united country, with the little Slav mini-states Lugansk and Donetsk in the East of Ukraine as being within Ukraine but having some degree of autonomy. Over eight long years Germany did not lift a finger to enforce this agreement. Instead, over eight long years these mini-republics have been shelled continually by the Kiev government, provoking an exodus of the populace into Russia. For a thousand years Russian-speaking Slav peoples had lived in this area, and Belarus and Russia both derived from this ancient *Rus* location, which grew around Kiev. Since the Neo-Nazi coup in 2014 a far-right ideology of racial purity has been endorsed: where the first act of the new parliament in Ukraine was to ban the Russian language, provoking Crimea to vote for its separation from Ukraine. The Russian-speaking Slavs were being treated as *Untermensch* by the Kiev government and an outright policy of ethnic cleansing was being pursued: endorsed by the West which has been supplying more deadly weapons to pursue this policy.

War as such began over February 16-17 of 2022 with a massive intensification of the shelling of the Donetsk region:

> You can see that **by the time Putin invaded Ukraine, the war had already begun.** The shelling of ethnic Russians had already intensified by many orders of magnitude. People were being slaughtered in droves, and tens of thousands of refugees were fleeing across the border into Russia. And, all of this had been going on since the 16th of February, a full week before Russia crossed the border.[209]

The OSCE recorded well over a thousand shells per day exploding in the Donetsk region. Do you remember how throughout December and January, we kept being given categorical assurances that Russia was

[209] unz.com/mwhitney/russia-started-the-war-and-other-fallacies/ 10.5.22

going to invade Ukraine? RT pundits denied this and were bemused by the claim. Lavrov didn't seem to know anything about it. *It was finally provoked by this sudden escalation.*

What do you call a country which continually shells its own people? The program was surely genocide as Putin stated, an ethnic cleansing program to remake the nation of Ukraine without its Slav component. The nations of Europe did not seem at all bothered by this. News outlets just omitted to report the cause of the conflict and who started it and when it began: they merely reported that on 24th of February Russian troops invaded the Ukraine – for no reason! Thereby the comic-book duality of good guys-bad guys was set up to goad Europe into anti-Russian hate.

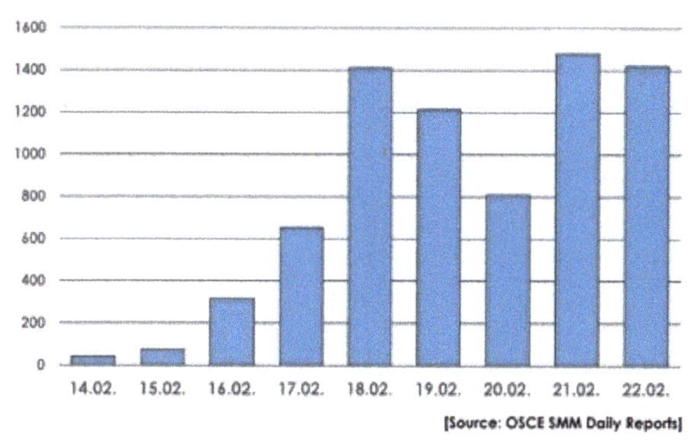

Figure: The war begins - OSCE data showing a hundred-fold increase in shelling over the Donbass area around 17th of February.

We note the critical sequence of events: a war of aggression began February 17th, then on 21st Russia *recognized* the two mini-states of 'People's Republics' then they responded by inviting Russia in, i.e. they requested aid. Russia had to invade the mainland of Ukraine because that was where the shelling was coming from. Considering that for eight years the main Kiev government had cut off Donetsk and Lugansk from electricity, water, banks, etc. one can say they were *de facto* independent states: also they were co-signators of the Minsk Agreement along with the Kiev government (plus Russia, France and Germany) which implies they reckoned a degree of autonomy. And so they surely had a right to make such a request. Here's military expert Scott Ritter:

> Russian President Vladimir Putin, citing Article 51 as his authority, ordered what he called a "special military operation".... **under Article 51, there can be no doubt as to the legitimacy of**

> **Russia's contention that the Russian-speaking population of the Donbass had been subjected to a brutal eight-year-long bombardment that had killed thousands of people....** Moreover, Russia claims to have **documentary proof that the Ukrainian Army was preparing for a massive military incursion into the Donbass** which was pre-empted by the Russian-led "special military operation."[210]

The long and short of the matter is that Russia has prevented the process of genocide and given the local Slav residents in Eastern Ukraine some hope for the future.

Europe does not seem to want anything except war. The British policy has been so successful. Already (2022) there are British SAS troops fighting with the Ukranian army. We will soon see how switching off the Russian gas will hurt Europe more than Russia.

Figure: main US-military Bio-labs in Ukraine, Kharkov top-right.

What is especially relevant for us is the sheer extent of US-funded bio-weapon research which Russian troops have uncovered in the Ukraine. The curtain is drawn back, to reveal that the NATO medical lab in Berlin which diagnosed 'Novichok' in the blood of Alexei Navalny (see page 142) had actually been working with US bio-warfare research in Ukraine, specifically at a site in Northern Ukraine right against the border of Russia. As Maria Zarakhova stated, "The Institute of Experimental and

[210] Mike Whitney, Ibid.

Clinical Veterinary Medicine in Kharkov has been the Institute of Microbiology of the German Armed Forces' main Ukrainian counterpart since 2016."[211]

The world should be grateful to Russia for uncovering these diabolical research labs and terminating them. The laboratories are entitled 'threat-reduction' bio-labs, reflecting a weakness in the Biological Weapons Convention: it bans all biological weapons, however it partially defines such in terms of *intention*: that they are designed with an intention to harm. It does not quite prohibit the development of such bio-weapon materials if it can be argued (or pretended) that the purpose is protective or medical or whatever. That is why Pentagon spokespersons believe they are not lying when they deny that America has got ongoing bio-weapons programs: which it has, of course. They are called Biological Threat Reduction programs. With bird species being trained to carry them over into Russia!

> Moscow claims Ukraine tried to infect the pro-Russian population in the Lugansk People's Republic with tuberculosis (TB) and allowed the Pentagon to carry out human experiments at Kharkov's psychiatric wards.

That is an RT news announcement - one can see why rt.com has been banned from most search-engines, and RT banned from TV, thereby preventing Britons from reaching a balanced view.

Russia's top CBW expert has claimed that Russian forces have obtained evidence suggesting Kiev attempted to infect residents of a district in the Lugansk People's Republic (LPR) with a highly pathogenic strain of tuberculosis in 2020. "Leaflets made in the form of counterfeit banknotes were infected with the causative agent of tuberculosis and distributed among minors in the village of Stepovoe," he stated, adding that the organizers of this crime took into account the behavior of children such as "putting things in their mouth and handling food without washing their hands.[212]

Russian officials also claimed that the Pentagon had conducted "inhumane" experiments on the patients of at least two

[211] english.almayadeen.net/news/politics/russia:-germany-involved-in-military-biological-activities-i

[212] rt.com/russia/555333-ukraine-biolabs-inhumane-experiments/

psychiatric institutions in Kharkov: "The main category of experimental subjects was a group of male, highly physically exhausted patients aged between 40 to 60 years," Kirillov said.

We thus gather, that during the entire Navalny hoax of 2020 the US was actually developing diabolical biological-warfare programs on Russia's border, and trying them out on groups of mental patients. The hypocrisy of European politicians is here quite breath-taking. The scenario seems to have come straight out of a 'Resident Evil' film script.

Only the truth can save us now. It is hard to think of any war that has involved so much deception, such manifest untruth. The US and Germany have been outrightly violating the Biological Weapons Convention, which they have signed and ratified.

At the time of writing (May 2022) Europe is choosing a future of poverty and war and is re-erecting a dismal Iron Curtain. It is hate that now unites NATO, hatred of Russia. The straight-from Hell US/UK fabricated terror events started with Litvinenko in 2006, going through to the still-unresolved MH-17 shootdown mystery of 2014, then Skripal 2018 and Navalny 2020: how well these deceptions have worked, in extinguishing the prospect of a prosperous Europe, at peace with itself. The expulsion of diplomats in the wake of these events was crucially important, in preventing peace. Now *homo exterminans* will be able to advise politicians of their strategic options and the *necro-technocrats* will get more funding, while *Those Who Create Delusion* get to write the press releases.

Under these circumstances the reader in invited to close her or his eyes and try to envisage Ministries of Peace. Who would fund them? These would be empathetic and would feel the pain of the Other. They would have to be composed of persons having an intelligence level capable of deconstructing the fabricated-terror events, whether real atrocities or just film-script setups. Anyone attempting to set up such non-government funded organizations should not expect gratitude; *au contraire* they should expect to be damned as useful idiots, unpatriotic, treasonous etc. However, the words of Jesus Christ would apply to them: 'Blessed are the peacemakers, for they shall be called the Children of God.'

Appendices

1

In 2018 the US Lyndon Larouche Foundation sent the following petition concerning the effect of the Steele Dossier to President Trump:

"The Congressional investigations into the origins of the ongoing, fake Russiagate coup against your presidency have revealed that the Obama Administration used false information and evidence fabricated in London, by official and unofficial British intelligence agents, to justify an unprecedented FBI counterintelligence investigation of your campaign.

Former MI6 agent Christopher Steele told his Department of Justice handler, former Associate Deputy Attorney General Bruce Ohr, that he would "do anything" to prevent Donald Trump's election and was desperate to stop it from happening. Steele was the author of the notorious fake dossier claiming that Donald Trump, having previously been sexually compromised by Vladimir Putin, was working with Putin to defeat Hillary Clinton. Steele's bizarre, amateurish, and totally fake dossier was used by a corrupted FBI to justify steps in its illegal investigation, despite the fact that this dossier was paid for by the Clinton campaign and its facts were unverified.

According to multiple published reports, Obama's CIA Director, John Brennan, convened an illegal intelligence task force at the CIA to launder and investigate fake dirt on Trump, produced by a British spy circle led by former MI6 chief Sir Richard Dearlove for purposes of destroying the Trump presidential campaign. Brennan did this because, he said, Donald Trump's election would jeopardize the "special relationship" between U.S. and British intelligence agencies. Dearlove had played a key role in the faked intelligence which led the United States into the Iraq War...

The British are conducting an international campaign to smear and militarily and economically confront Russia and China because the City of London financial and imperial order is economically and morally bankrupt and has no plan to build a future for humanity over the course of the next 50 years. This British campaign is not in the interest of the United States, and, Mr. President, you were elected in substantial part on the promise to end America's useless wars on behalf of British strategic objectives."

The Larouche Foundation commented on the story:[213]

---

213 larouchepac.com 'President Trump: Declassify all Documents & Information Concerning

"The liberated documents show that Sir Andrew Wood and Pablo Miller, Sergei Skripal's MI6 handler, who are both players in Christopher Steele's *Orbis Business Intelligence,* also have significant relationships to the Initiative. Skripal and his daughter were poisoned in Salisbury, England, in one of 2018's more infamous intelligence hoaxes targeting Russia. Steele, of course, wrote the very dirty and obviously fake dossier on Donald Trump and Vladimir Putin which has sustained the Russiagate scandal for almost two years in the United States, throwing this country into a McCarthyite hysteria…"

At the center of the Institute's very military operations, is the use of propaganda directed simultaneously at both the government and the general population. Institute personnel lobby governments on behalf of war-party policies against Russia and China, for example, in their disguise as private parties, while the Institute itself is being paid, as a think-tank, by the very same governments. At the same time, the Institute's media contacts echo the entirely concocted government "debate" to the general population. This circular churning of the media sphere is what Obama's former security advisor Ben Rhodes called creating a public opinion "echo chamber." Rhodes cut his national security chops by helping with production of the fraud known as the 9/11 Commission Report. This methodology, fully implemented in the British propaganda and regime change operation against Putin, which began with the Litvinenko poisoning in 2006 and dramatically escalated in 2014, has created an astounding and deranged war fever against Putin in Britain and throughout Europe."

2

An idiot's guide to the Skripal affair

by *Panopticon,*

at The Syrian Observatory for Human Wrongs,

here reproduced with kind permission

A sad, funny story of Sergei and Yulia –
not 'funny ha-ha', but funny peculiar…
One Sunday in March they decided to eat

British Subversion of your Campaign;' also Larouche, 'Russiagate Is Being Transformed into an Exposure of the British Coup,' Jan 2019.

at a nice little café, then stopped at a seat
where they both felt unwell at the very same minute –
now I think that's quite a coincidence, 'innit?
So an ambulance came for the pair, as requested.
But when they were studied, and prodded, and tested,
nefarious substances in them were found –
and not only there, but spread all around
old Salisbury town, up hill and down valley –
(the High Street is now known as 'Chemical Alley').
A passing D.S. who just happened to be there,
was poisoned like them when he went off to see where
they lived – or did he succumb at the scene?
(His bosses told two different stories on screen).
And while a good nurse who had tended them well
suffered no side effects, 'far as I can tell,
some thirty-eight people were treated as victims,
but I think that someone was taking the mick, since
a day or two after those numbers were stated
the whole bloody lot of them evaporated.
*** Hmm. ***
The media descended like swivel-eyed dervishes,
paid no attention to church Sunday services;
campanologists' melodies had to be quietened,
so BBC viewers could all be enlightened:
"Could you silence those chimes, my parochial friend?"
"Well I could, but at least can we hear the bell end?"
Now Boris mistakenly took that as cue
to appear on the telly, and give us his view
that the case had been cracked by his government sources,
e'en though the police had advised "Hold your horses";
his bods back at Whitehall had worked round the clock
to identify something called 'Doorknobichok' TM
which he claimed had been smeared on the victims' front door,
under cover of darkness on March 3 or 4.
'Twas a devilish stuff that will kill you in seconds,
and was put there by Russkies (or so his boss reckons).
So lethal that only a tenth of a gram
would transport you to heaven, to visit your gran.
"So we have two deceased?" the reporters surmised;

"No, they're not dead" said Boris, "just hoskripalised!".
*** I thank you. ***
Then someone observed something really quite odd –
that the door didn't seem to have bothered the plod
who was tasked with the duty of guarding the place,
long before it was clear that a poison was traced.
"So how could this be?" it was asked of the Tory,
who conferred with his bosses, and then changed his story:
"No, it wasn't the handle, but gas-tainted air
in the Skripals' jalopy, 'cause Vlad put it there!"
Then when this didn't wash, he tried yet another –
"it was smuggled from Moscow by Yulia's mother! (in law)"
In one last attempt to convince us that Putin
had ordered his henchmen to go put the boot in:
"They may have consumed it at breakfast, you see –
in Ricincles or Special K(GB);
for although it would seem like the plot of a thriller,
I'm convinced that our Vlad is a cereal killer!"
*** Hmmm. ***
Then a cordon was thrown around Salisbury town,
which was only a bus ride from old Porton Down
(a village connected to our alleged traitor –
for Sergei is he – but more of that later).
The government said that their duty of care,
because of the obvious dangers in there
meant they might have to pull down the café and pub,
so the locals would have to go elsewhere for grub;
And because of the contaminated front door,
their dwelling might need to be razed to the floor.
Well, this understandably raised some concerns
with the Salisbury folk, who took it in turns
to request some advice, because nobody knows
if they'd gotten the stuff on their shoes, or their clothes:
"Should we burn our belongings, or dump them at sea?"
"Nah, just wash 'em on 'quick rinse' at forty degrees".
"And what of that sinister place up the lane
where your poisons are made, is that whence it came?"
"If you don't mind me saying, your question's absurd,
as of Doorknobichok TMay, we never have heard,

except for the stockpiles we keep for ourselves,
and they are all safe and secure on our shelves".
*** Oops. ***
The blame was laid squarely on Moscow and Vlad
(as we know from our Bond films that Russians are bad);
expulsion of diplomats worldwide arranged;
accusations thrown, and insults exchanged.
All cultural visits were cancelled or put off,
and Julie Assange had his internet cut off.
Then lo! and behold, our story got murky,
in a village you'll find in a country near Turkey.
The Syrian leader, one Bashar Assad,
was repelling invaders, which made the West mad;
but just as his victory was nearing at last,
his own population he cruelly gassed –
or so we were told by the Powers That Be,
who strung us a line, didn't want us to see
that some brave independents were taking a risk,
like Bartlett and Beeley, Stuart and Fisk,
to show us the true situation in Douma –
if the press did its job we'd have realised sooner
that far from Assad being a monster, and hated
by all of his people, he was celebrated
and trusted to stand up as their only true hope,
in the face of attacks from the U.S. and Europe.
And he wasn't a 'butcher', on murderous mission,
but a family man, and a licenced optician.
*** We should've gone to Specsavers. ***
Emotional images filled up our screens,
showing suffering women, and babies, and teens;
they were choking on chlorine, which made us all furious –
but no men affected, which did seem quite curious…
The West didn't wait, we accepted the claim
that the evil Assad was entirely to blame.
He was guilty of war crimes, as evidence proved –
for the good of the people, he must be removed!
Notwithstanding the signs that the Syrians may seem
broadly in favour of Mr. A's 'regime'
and the fact that with Russia they had some protection

from outside attacks, or their own insurrection.
Our Washington friends would insist that they need some
of Uncle Sam's good ol' American freedom
which had been so successful, I'm frequently told,
where nations had hardships, and oil, gas, and gold.
The narrative blaming Assad for the crimes
was reported as fact in The Sun and The Times
and most western leaders were keen to appease the
hawkish intentions of Boris and Theresa.
But a doubt did remain that the entire event
might have been a 'false flag', with malicious intent –
would our lovable 'BoJo' condone such a stunt?
Yes he would, because he's an untrustworthy cad....

****

Before we continue I think that we ought'ta
return to the poor stricken father and daughter
whose problems all started when they were infected
with poison – but how this event was connected
to wider concerns internationally,
and the threat of an outbreak of World War III
can be found in the c.v. of old Mister S.,
and the time he was caught and was made to confess
that a Brit double-agent was his part-time job,
with some colleagues betrayed for a few extra bob.
So a jail cell in Moscow was where he would stay,
till a spy swap arrangement took him to U.K.
Here he stayed for a while, but he yearned to go home,
which worried the spooks listening in on his phone.
Was this why the homesick old Russian was nobbled?
Or was it the claim that with help he had cobbled
together a dossier aimed at the POTUS,
that the Democrats hoped would dissuade U.S. voters
And result in the triumph of Hillary Clinton,
with subsequent guaranteed hell, fire and brimstone?
The plot didn't work, and old Trump was elected,
but whatever the reason the pair were infected,
our government said "It's clear if you ask us,
that this can be traced all the way to Damascus,
for it shows that the Russians will use any measure

to help young Assad and incur our displeasure;
The agents of Putin can poison to order
And will have no respect for law, life or border.
But nothing must stop the success of our plan
which began in Baghdad and will end in Tehran."
*** "Highly Likely" ***
So despite all the evidence proving this crisis
was carefully staged by the West's friends in ISIS,
these facts were ignored by the Beeb and the papers,
who called for an end to the Syrian's capers.
This gave our P.M. all the reasons she needed
to mount an attack, with all protests unheeded,
along with her chums in the U.S. and France,
but they thoughtfully notified Vlad in advance;
for this wasn't a true act of war, but a sham,
to convince all the voters that they had a plan.
A fortune was spent on some shiny new rockets
(replacements would benefit shareholders' pockets);
so where shall we fire 'em? Mrs. May scratched her head:
"Well we wouldn't want anyone injured, or dead,
but we know where he hides his consignment of gases,
to terrorise all of his downtrodden masses,
so we'll send in these missiles, with shock and with awe,
and we'll blow the dumps up, which will shorten the war".
"Won't those missiles release all the toxins therein,
to kill one and all – a terrible sin??"
A blank look appeared, then Theresa retorted:
"I'd not thought of that, could you please not report it?"
*** Jesus H. Christ. ***
The bombing commenced, on irrelevant target
So the Maybot could emulate her idol, Margaret,
and show that in conflict she was strong and mighty
but meanwhile, something was stirring in Blighty.....
Our young Russian lady, whose certain demise
was expected, suddenly opened her eyes
just as Easter approached, in her hospital prison,
To be greeted with cries of "Christ, she is risen!"
And to make matters worse, she had borrowed a phone
and confirmed her good health to her cousin back home –

which scuppered the prospect that Yulia could
have been quietly forgotten, or silenced for good.
But what of her daddy, who'd been at death's door
'cause he'd got on the outside of A-234?
Well I'm glad to report that, despite the prognosis
that follows ingestion of such fatal doses
both he and the bobby awoke from their comas,
which filled sceptics' nostrils with fishy aromas;
for what kind of poison, designed to be lethal
has no such effect on these three lucky people?
There were so many questions we needed to ask,
but journalists didn't seem up to the task;
this global concern that had Doomsday advancing
took a sad second place behind 'Strictly Come Dancing'.
And the government proved they had something to hide
by imposing a ban on reporting worldwide.
*** Russians can dance too! ***
So the Skripals survived , but we still couldn't see them,
the Powers That Be had denied them their freedom
And took them away to location unknown
without access to newspapers, TV or phone.
(I thought that their chances were now slim-to-none –
remember the plotline of 'Capricorn One'?)
Then just as our hopes had been starting to fade
our Yulie appeared in a green English glade
and read out a statement, author unknown,
that asked if we kindly would leave her alone;
for although she was well she would like to appeal
that we give her more time to get through her ordeal;
and this sentiment really had nothing to do
with the fact that her kidnappers bloody well knew
that if they could escape from their new adversaries
they'd scoot back to Moscow and sing like canaries.
For if you think that Russia was guilty, I'll tell you
where we can meet up, there's a bridge I can sell you…

Epilogue

So that was the last that we saw of the pair
but it isn't the end of this sorry affair

For although we're not sure why the Skripals were picked on
It's clear the official response was pure fiction
and twisted to play to the NeoCons' plan
to annihilate Syria, to get to Iran
and to demonise Russia, who stands in the way
of a world dominated by U.S. of A.
Who'd support this assault? The U.K. and E.U. did
and lied through their teeth, 'cause they think we're all stupid.
But the crimes we commit on behalf of our rotten
regimes to our neighbours, will not be forgotten;
their patience will only protect us so far
then the West will provoke an unwinnable war.
And we'll wonder how things could have got to the state
where we fear for ourselves and our own children's fate
but forget that this land, where democracy lives
is now governed by liars, and traitors, and spivs
who will rig the roulette wheel for guaranteed wins
till we find that they've played us like cheap violins;
whose fake manifestos fight for our attention
with lies about justice, and healthcare, and pensions;
who'll cheat, kill and steal, till they've conquered all nations
preaching hatred of Africans, Russians and Asians
and throughout their pursuits they'll accept no dissent
and it's all on behalf of the great one per cent.
And we'll ask God how He could allow such a sin
And He'll say "It was you lot who voted them in."

Acronyms used

CW Chemical weapons

ECHR European Court of Human Rights

FCO Foreign and Commonwealth Office

FSB Federal Security Service, Russian

FVEY Five Eyes – UK ,US, Canada, Australia & N.Z. Intel.

GCHQ Government Communications HeadQuarters

NGO Non-Governmental Organization

OPCW Organis^{n} for Prevention of Chemical Weapons

OSCE Organis^{n} for Security and Co-operation in Europe

TASS Russian news service

Index

www.ingramcontent.com/pod-product-compliance
Lightning Source LLC
Chambersburg PA
CBHW041219030426
42336CB00024B/3397
* 9 7 8 1 7 3 9 9 9 4 1 4 *